Polity Press

108 Cowley Road OXFORD OX4 1J Tel: 0865 791100

REVIEW COPY

TITLE: ESCAPE FROM THE BASTILLE

AUTHOR: QUETEL

PRICE: hb £29.50   pb

ISBN: hb 0745605 966   pb

PUBLICATION DATE: 14.5.90

For further information contact publicity manager   Rebbeca Harkin   on 0865

The publisher requests that no review should appear before the publication date and that your review simultaneously both editions if published in hardback and paperback. Please send two copies of the

Escape from the Bastille

The Life and Legend of Latude

Claude Quétel

Translated by Christopher Sharp

Polity Press

English translation © Polity Press 1990
First published in France as *Les Évasions de Latude*
Copyright © by éditions Denoël 1986

First published 1990 by Polity Press
in association with Basil Blackwell

Editorial office:
Polity Press
65 Bridge Street,
Cambridge CB2 1UR, UK

Marketing and production:
Basil Blackwell Ltd
108 Cowley Road, Oxford OX4 1JF, UK

ISBN 0 7456 0596 6

British Library Cataloguing in Publication Data
A CIP catalogue record for this book is available from the
British Library.

Typeset in 12 on 14 pt. Bembo
by Photo·Graphics, Honiton, Devon
Printed in Great Britain by T. J. Press, Padstow

Contents

Appendixes

1

The Booby-trap Parcel

In the stagecoach bringing him back to Paris, a young man contemplated the flat Flemish countryside moving past. The Treaty of Aix-la-Chapelle, which had just been signed in that month of October 1748, had put an end to his employment as assistant surgeon to the itinerant army hospital. He was twenty-three years old and now found himself a civilian again. All his worldly possessions consisted of a few hundred *livres*, which he had saved up coin by coin, a large trunk full of clothes and a letter of recommendation for Marshal de Noailles's personal surgeon.

He was of average height, somewhat slender and endowed by nature with a pleasant, cheerful face. He wore a short, slightly curly and carefully powdered wig. Girls found him attractive despite a few scars left over from a bout of chickenpox, which had aged him prematurely, and despite his awful Gascon accent which betrayed his provincial background. This would not have mattered if he had been of respectable birth, but he was all too well aware of the fact that his name, Jean Danry, was not a real one. Born in Montagnac, in the Languedoc region, of Jeanneton Aubrespy and an unknown father, he was an illegitimate child and so had only a Christian name, Jean Henri, which he had changed to Jean Danry to cover up his bastard origin.

His mother, from a family of the middle bourgeoisie, but immediately rejected by her relatives, had brought him up single-handed, depriving herself of many comforts to do so. Sewing, weaving, engaging in tireless activity and affection, Jeanneton even succeeded in providing her son with some schooling. And now that he was seventeen, his father, seized by pangs of remorse, had turned his mind to setting him up. He was of noble birth and had taken part in various campaigns at the end of Louis XIV's reign. Married and father of six children, he lived quite poorly himself not far from there, in the Château de Creissels. He held the Order of Saint Louis. His name was Henry Vissec de Latude.

But what could he do with a boy, however bright and intelligent, who had no name? M. de Latude categorically ruled out recognizing the fruit of this youthful folly. A military career seemed the most obvious, but it was reserved for the nobility. Nevertheless, our young man could enter the army through the back door, with the humble rank of assistant surgeon. His career had begun in 1742 with the Languedoc army where he learned to perform bleedings (the major part of his task), and also to apply bandages, pull out teeth and shave beards. After the campaign in Alsace, where he had accompanied Marshal de Noailles's troops, he straight away rejoined the armies in Flanders. Well thought of by his superiors, in early 1748, after seven years of hard campaigns, Jean Danry was still an assistant surgeon earning the modest salary of 50 *livres* a month.

In short, he was a young man, quite unknown, on his way to confront the great city of Paris.

Six months later Jean Danry was to be found living in furnished accommodation, on the Cul-de-sac du Coq, where he shared a dark, dirty room with a chemist's apprentice called Jean-Baptiste Binguet. As was to be the case with many of his kind, life in Paris had gobbled up the young man's savings within a few months. Easy women, dinners, an ever-growing number of friends to treat had forced him to leave the modest, but comfortable, hotel he had originally occupied and go to live on the Cul-de-sac du Coq where many young people like him, newly arrived from their own province, or sometimes deserters, struggled along nursing their hopes for a thousand plans and living off small temporary jobs, if not by their wits. The letter of recommendation and many attempts to find employment proved fruitless. There was no demand for assistant surgeons. In any case, Jean Danry had ambitions other than holding a pan for bleeding. Did he not after all have noble blood in him?

In the meantime, his funds were beginning to run dangerously low and the rent for his room, paltry as it was, had not been paid for several weeks. Here was Danry faced with the possibility of being thrown out into the street, his old rags confiscated. A request for money from his mother, who was still living in Montagnac, had informed him of a fact that he should have already known, which was that the poor woman was barely able to provide for herself. He wrote another letter to the quartermaster of the Flanders armies claiming that he had been stripped of his money and his belongings at the siege of Berg-Op-Zoom and was therefore entitled to compensation. This late request was in itself a sufficient sign of fraud, and the army quartermaster's assistants did not even bother to reply.

Hence it was that on the evening of 26 April 1749, with gloomy thoughts racing through his head, Jean Danry walked alone after dinner in the Jardin des Tuileries. The park was a popular spot for strollers, but also attracted adventurers of all kinds. The sad-looking boy, forever dressed in a grey suit and red coat, had also become a regular habitué of the place where perhaps, by a miracle, he might meet someone to help him out of his dire straits. As he ambled down a path, he lent an ear to the various conversations. As it did every evening, talk centred on the fight at Court between the Marquise de Pompadour and the ministers. It seemed that the 'King's whore' (as she was referred to here), whose disgrace had already been announced months ago, was well and truly at work strengthening her position. And yet, hadn't there been a time when she had feared being poisoned?

Danry was sitting down not far from two men talking like this about the Pompadour and not concealing their hatred for the favourite. They barely lowered their voices at the sight of Danry, for it was obvious that he was not one of the many police spies at large in the capital. Danry listened to the suggestive jokes: 'The bitch must be really talented for the King to keep her in spite of everything!'

Danry listened, but he also thought with growing excitement that fate was beckoning him on. He pictured himself running to Versailles and warning the Marquise de Pompadour. It didn't matter if she already knew, as was certainly the case, that she was surrounded by hatred. Whoever gave her true and useful advice could certainly hope for some protection and eventually an occupation . . . The two individuals had already left some time ago, as Danry continued to think about this unique opportunity offered to him. To go and inform the Marquise that there were people who did not like her, or even that she was running risks, would surely be ridiculous. But why not warn her of more precise danger, plotted in all its details?

After a sleepless night of conjuring up crazy ideas, Danry stopped his planning. He ran under the arches of the Palais-Royal to buy six of those small very fine glass bottles called 'Batavian tears' from a vendor in that area. Children – and grown-ups – spent their time breaking the hooked end, so as to make a loud crack. From another vendor he bought a few pennies' worth of powder, alum and (harmless) powdered vitriol. Finally, he went to a stationer in the Rue Saint-Honoré, and bought some thick paper.

Hastily returning to his room, he put four of the phials (two had already broken) into a parcel of his own making, inserting a piece of string through the hooks, which he attached to a lid after covering the whole with a layer of powders he had mixed himself, thus producing a bluish colour. When the parcel was opened, the bottles would break and release the odour of what would seem to be a subtle poison. On the box, he wrote: 'Madame, please open this package with particular care.' Thick paper covered the false booby-trap parcel which Danry addressed 'to Madame la Marquise de Pompadour, at Court'.

The next day, on 28 April, after last-minute hesitations, Danry went to deposit his package at the main post office and immediately left on foot for Versailles. He arrived there extremely late, about midnight, and asked at once to see Mme de Pompadour in person on business of the utmost importance. The valets, however, were used to hearing this kind of story hundreds of times a day and were quite already onto the scent of intrigue, especially since it was late, even for Versailles. He insisted, though, and was able to speak with the head valet, who agreed to listen to his story:

While walking through the Jardin des Tuileries the night before, around eight o'clock, and going behind the bushes to relieve himself of a pressing need, Danry overheard the conversation of two men dressed in black, wearing swords. 'Well, did you do it?' the first man asked. 'Yes, it's in hand', answered the second, 'I'll be hanged if the King kisses her tomorrow!' Danry then followed them and saw them taking the package to the main post office. Devoted to the interests of the Marquise, he had rushed to reveal

what he had seen, and especially to warn her not to open
the package herself, for it might be dangerous.

To understand the effect produced by such a statement, it
is important to take a look at the state of mind at Court in
April 1749. Since the death of Cardinal de Fleury six years
earlier, Louis XV had been governing France himself, in
financial difficulties aggravated by the recent War of
Succession with Austria and the failure to implement a new
tax (the *vingtième*, a twentieth of one's income), which was
to have affected all without exception. Court expenditure
was therefore at the height of unpopularity, and in particular
that attributed to the King's official mistress since 1745,
Mme de Pompadour.

   In 1749 Jeanne-Antoinette was twenty-eight. She was at
the height of her beauty, not to mention her education,
grace, intelligence and even her distinction. She and the
King were still madly in love. But she was surrounded by
enemies! The daughter of a gallant mother, the protégée of
a tax farmer whose nephew she had married, not only was
she born outside the noble class, but in addition her name
was Poisson, meaning 'fish' in French. This accounted for
the unflattering 'poissonnades' composed against the 'King's
whore'; these were satirical songs which, to say the least,
were aimed 'below the belt'. Nevertheless, those who
favoured, and sometimes even orchestrated, such sentiments
were prominent people. Thus the Duc de Richelieu and the
Comte de Maurepas, Secretary of State to the King's
Household and the Navy . . .

   The past five years had witnessed a testing duel between
Mme de Pompadour and Minister Maurepas, most often in
the Marquise's favour. However, in 1749, the Marquise had
finally triumphed over her enemies, and more particularly
over the Comte de Maurepas whose disgrace she was to

bring about in August. In parallel to this, 'Her Majesty Cotillon III' (as Frederick II of Prussia called her) grew in influence in the world of art and politics. The Marquise de Pompadour dictated letters and received a growing number of supplicants. Ministers soon were to become accustomed to meeting the King about the affairs of the realm in his private rooms.

So the effect caused by Danry's action may be judged. To threaten the Marquise de Pompadour was tantamount to threatening what the King cherished most, and such information had to be taken seriously. Therefore, when the parcel arrived in Versailles on the afternoon of 29 April, a thrill of emotion went through the Marquise's circle. The King's physician, Quesnay himself, was asked to open it. He did so with the utmost caution, only to find the harmless mixture described previously. The little bottles did not even explode. Nevertheless, the presence of vitriol, a harmful substance, gave greater weight to the theory of a clumsy, but real, attempt at poisoning than to the idea of a simple bad joke. The King and his favourite were informed and could not conceal a degree of fear. In short, the false parcel was becoming a real affair of state.

The Marquise de Pompadour, disillusioned and hardened by the struggles, often sordid, that pitted her against her enemies, now saw a chance to let her faithful ally Berryer, lieutenant-general of the Paris police, deploy his not inconsiderable zeal. As for Minister d'Argenson, who had Berryer under his wing, but who had supported Maurepas for a long time, it was in his entire interest to shed light on the affair as soon as possible now that the winds were shifting in favour of the King's favourite. In this context, the booby-trap parcel was a godsend, even if it turned out to be harmless. Actually, it was a prelude to the repression that would not fail to fall mercilessly on the satirists who insulted Mme de Pompadour. As time went on, even an

indirect pamphlet of the type 'I salute you, Queen bitch
. . .' or an 'African story or the life of Melotta Ossompay',
would lead their authors straight to the Bastille.

The brains behind the plot had to be found and severely
punished, and the informer would be given a reward. But
where was the informer? The valet who had received Danry
the night before had to admit with embarrassment that he
had encouraged the man to leave, reluctant to admit such
a strange individual to the waiting room. Luckily, this same
man had left his name and address in the quite legitimate
hope of a reward. The police chief chose the most capable
and intelligent of his officers, police officer Saint-Marc,
with authority to conduct the investigation and to be on
the lookout for Danry with all speed.

The same day, Saint-Marc went to Paris and questioned
Danry, who repeated the story of the two men dressed in
black. However, in the eighteenth century, thanks to the
creation of a lieutenant-general of the Paris police at the
beginning of Louis XIV's reign, the police force was
well organized. Superintendents and inspectors virtually
controlled the capital. They were kept informed by hundreds
of spies (popularly called *mouches* in French, literally 'flies')
and were assisted by nearly a thousand secretaries, exempts
(police officers), archers (arresting officers) and guards. One
man alone directed this enormous machine as absolute
master. The lieutenant-general of police had only to account
to the minister of the King's Household, if not to the King
himself.

Hence Danry had barely spoken of those mysterious men
in black before Saint-Marc was already sending out their
description that same evening of the 29th to police officers
who were soon maintaining surveillance over the capital's
public parks. Now, if any men in black corresponding to

Danry's description of the two individuals had been seen, in the Jardins du Luxembourg and the Jardins du Palais-Royal in particular, none of them was carrying a sword. Consequently, no shadowing was undertaken.

But Saint-Marc was an intelligent policeman, and at the same time was gathering information about the case's only witness. He was informed that the man had a reputation for being quite a liar, that he was quite well acquainted with Paris, a professional gambler often visiting prostitutes and sometimes involved in brawls. Moreover, Danry had not wanted the police officer to accompany him to his room. Now when Saint-Marc questioned the landlord, he was told that another young man lived there and worked, coincidentally, in an apothecary suitable for supplying the powders used to make up the parcel.

Saint-Marc's suspicions rapidly grew to the point of conviction. On 30 April, only twenty-four hours after the false booby-trap parcel had been delivered to Versailles, Saint-Marc made his report to the chief of police, Berryer, and concluded: 'All things considered, I believe that Danry is the chief character in this business. It is highly possible that this Gascon libertine, at the end of all his resources, made up the whole story with Binguet, the apothecary, believing that by going to Versailles himself to bring so clear a warning to the Marquise de P. he would receive a sizeable reward.' And then Saint-Marc recommended that Danry and Binguet should be arrested and undergo separate interrogation, and that their room should be searched.

Berryer had complete confidence in his subordinate who would not indeed have prepared this report lightly. So he proposed that the King issue a *lettre de cachet*. Swift action had to be taken in order to be able to unmask accomplices. Now the *lettre de cachet* precisely allowed swift action, and that was why it was created. It was no illegal or shameful instrument, but an institution set up whereby the King exercised his legal right. So *lettres de cachet* began with the words 'De par le Roy' (meaning 'upon decision of the King') and were signed 'Louis'.

Actually, in eighteenth-century France and in Paris, this convenient method was for the most part under the control of the lieutenant-general of police. One of Paris's most famous chiefs of police, d'Argenson (the father of the minister in office in 1749), used to say that frequent recourse to the *lettre de cachet*, that is, to the King's authority which no one could or would imagine contesting, was the 'common source of its weakness'. He explained that 'common justice often gives licence to the greatest crimes because of the laxity of case law, and this is also what forces me on such occasions to have recourse to the immediate authority of the King who alone makes our criminals tremble and who remains untouched by ingenious subterfuges and the know-how of chicanery.'

But this extraordinary justice remained justice, at least in the spirit of the *ancien régime*. Besides, it was the King himself who decided whether or not to issue a *lettre de cachet*, especially in a case like that of this booby-trap parcel where one way or another his immediate circle had been threatened. In fact, the crime of *lèse-majesté* remained, even if it had been proved that the parcel was harmless. Was there not the risk of this being the work of a madman whose ignorance and clumsiness had been the only obstacles to the creation of a truly dangerous contrivance?

Under Louis XIV, guards or servants who thought themselves clever by alluding to the King's safety ('If I wanted to . . .') were already being sent to the Bastille, at least for a period of questioning. After the poison case, suspicion was on the rise. A chambermaid who had wanted to attract attention by pretending to have been poisoned was locked up in prison for a long time. In 1684 a footman to the ambassador of Venice had had the bright idea in a waiting room at Versailles of saying: 'What's to stop me from going to kill the King?' He was sent straight to the Bastille by *lettre de cachet,* and for good measure the ambassador's other valet was also sent there although he had only had the bad luck to be listening. As for that King's guard, who had cut himself slightly with a knife to make everyone believe that he had repelled an attack and thus to receive a reward for it, he was sent to the Bastille, sentenced and hanged. Keen concern for the King's safety was such that even imaginary plots and false informers ended up being harshly suppressed.

That was why on 1 May, that is, less than forty-eight hours after the arrival of the parcel, police officer Saint-Marc left Versailles with a *lettre de cachet* addressed to the governor of the Bastille: 'Monsieur de Launay, I send you this letter to instruct you to take the men called Danry, an assistant surgeon, and Binguet, an apothecary's apprentice, into my castle, the Bastille, and to keep them there until further instructions from me. May God, Monsieur de Launay, have you under his holy protection. Written in Marly on 1 May 1749 (signed 'Louis', countersigned by De Voyer d'Argenson).'

However, at that time, although the dreaded *lettre de cachet* was hovering over Danry's head, while he was still persuaded that royal compensation would soon raise him from his lowly position, sufficient proof had not yet been found to establish his guilt solidly. But that was not important. The Bastille was not solely a place for the notoriously seditious, but also for suspects who, once locked up, could be interrogated at leisure and if in the end found innocent, just released a few weeks later.

At the end of Louis XIV's reign, there had already been a case surprisingly similar to Danry's: 'The King', the minister of the King's Household wrote at that time, 'is sending to the castle of the Bastille a man whose only crime is to have informed me that he has something very important to reveal regarding the King's person and the State and that he would only transmit such information in person to His Majesty. I tried to make him speak, but it was to no avail. This leads me to believe . . . that poverty and the poor state of his affairs have driven him to invent this imaginary warning, in the hope of some reward. We thought it best to lock him up in the Bastille and make him suffer, to force him to reveal his information or his imposture . . .'

The same precaution in Danry's case. The King gave his approval and asked to be informed personally of the outcome of the interrogation. And then if the matter remained obscure, Danry's own guilt would be beyond doubt. In fact, following his intuition, the intelligent Saint-Marc had got Danry to write out his statement. He had just compared its writing to that on the parcel. It was the same.

2

At the Bastille

About eight o'clock in the evening on that same day of 1 May Saint-Marc and a few arresting officers arrived at the Cul-de-sac du Coq. Danry was put into a carriage without any explanation and taken straight to the Bastille. His fellow lodger Binguet received the same treatment a few minutes later.

With its eight enormous towers connected to one another by an equally imposing wall, the 24-metre-high Bastille dominated Paris's Saint-Antoine district. In the latter part of the Middle Ages the structure served as a military citadel to defend the Saint-Antoine gate. It then became the Chamber of the Treasury in Sully's day. It was not long, however, before the royal power started to use it to lock up prisoners: conspirators, spies, criminals, counterfeiters, madmen . . . Since the reign of Louis XIII the Bastille had been used solely as a state prison together with some forty other castles and citadels throughout the realm, such as the Château d'If, Mont-Saint-Michel, the Castle-keep of Vincennes, etc. But the Bastille was by far the most awe-inspiring, and when an important person happened to disappear suddenly, it was easy to say that he had been sent to the Bastille.

A maximum of forty or fifty prisoners, all sent there by *lettre de cachet*, were distributed in large circular rooms built into each of these towers. From the end of the Middle Ages up to the Revolution, nearly 6,000 were to have been 'bastilled' (Voltaire coined the word *embastiller*, 'to bastille' in English, when he himself became acquainted with the famous prison in 1717). And it was in the reign of Louis XV that the number of detainees in the Bastille increased. Nobles and commoners alike were dispatched there for political reasons, embezzlement, violations of the press, on religious grounds, in police cases, not to mention insanity, witchcraft, duels or impertinence at Court.

Nevertheless, in the mind of the government at least, imprisonment at the Bastille was a favour, and many did not 'deserve' to be placed there, whether on account of their low social rank or because of the wrong they were accused of committing. In both cases the Bastille, like the other state prisons, offered conditions of discretion and security superior to those of other detention centres spread over the realm (convents, general hospitals) where the dregs of delinquency and second-class citizens were dumped. The Bastille had a more distinguished batch of individuals who more often than not were financiers who had robbed the State beyond accepted limits rather than cut-throats. This indicated to what extent the case of the booby-trap parcel was taken seriously.

Once over the drawbridge, Danry, totally demoralized by this set-back, was led through the admission procedures. In order to ensure that the prisoner could not retain anything on his person, he was searched thoroughly from head to foot, stripped of his clothes and his papers and other personal belongings. He was made to change into fresh clothes, albeit threadbare, which was the attire in use at the Bastille. It basically consisted of an ill-fitting pair of trousers, a long shirt and a large hooded dressing-gown, all complete

with large slippers, a pair of coarse socks and a ludicrous
cap. In a silence interrupted only by the curt instructions
of the officers present, Danry's name was then entered in
the Bastille register and next he was led to one of the large
rooms in what had been nicknamed the Corner Tower. A
double door, reinforced by heavy iron bars, was closed
after him without any attention being paid to his anguished
questions. He found himself alone.

The next day, the lieutenant-general of police came in
person to interrogate him. This was, to a certain degree,
the privilege of prisoners at the Bastille. Berryer was still
a young man (he was only forty-four years old) and had
been in his important position only for the past two years.
He therefore wanted to show himself equal to his duties.
It was particularly important in this case, as Minister
d'Argenson was waiting for him in Marly to hear personally
the report that he himself would repeat to the King. But
Berryer was an honest and kind man and was quite ready
to admit that Danry had been the victim of a hoax. He was
particularly intelligent and he knew that only patience would
let him get to the bottom of the mysterious case. He
therefore approached the prisoner with the utmost courtesy,
showing that he was distressed that higher authorities had
obliged him to decide on the Bastille. But it was up to the
prisoner to find a way out by proving his innocence or by
denouncing possible associates.

So Danry once again repeated his story of the men in
black, proclaimed his innocence and complained of the
injustice being done to him. Was this the reward he was
entitled to expect for his devotion to the Marquise de
Pompadour? Berryer felt sorry for the rather nice young
man, who had just lost a unique opportunity of clearing
himself. He tried to make Danry understand in persuasive
terms that this story no longer held up, since his handwriting
had been identified on the parcel. Danry then become angry

and thereafter confined himself to silence, which led the lieutenant-general of police to believe that there really had been a plot with many ramifications.

Since he could or would not talk, Danry started to write. Isolation from the outside world at the Bastille was relative and more often than not the prisoners could correspond with the authorities and, in most cases, with anyone else, but the content of the letters was, of course, first examined.

Efforts were even made to satisfy a prisoner's little whims, such as bringing a prisoner his violin from home. Thus, when Danry asked to have his clothes back from the laundress, someone was sent to ask for them, with the hope that some item of proof might perhaps be found.

In his letters, Danry desperately stuck to his initial statement and on 9 May, when he found out that Berryer was leaving for Versailles, he wrote to him: 'I dare take the liberty, dear Sir, to request that you kindly ask about me when in the presence of those who are keeping me locked up here. If I dare ask you this favour – of going to see Mme la Marquise de Pompadour and telling her that I beg her pardon if I did wrong in going to Versailles to inform her of what I had heard in the Tuileries and what I had seen these two men doing when they went to the post office, I thought I was doing right by telling her everything . . . and that I do not believe I have deserved such treatment . . .' In another letter, however, he showed himself to be more sibylline, and was content to write: 'I'm at the Bastille, but it's not for theft or murder. I hope the case will soon be over.'

After a fortnight Danry finally decided to tell the simple truth. He described his extreme misery and how he had thought up the idea of the incredible stratagem. But he would have preferred death to hatching a plot capable of harming anyone at all, still less Mme la Marquise de Pompadour. He went on to explain that the materials enclosed in the small parcel were totally harmless. In any case, he had not received advice or help from anyone, nor had he spoken to anyone about the matter. Paradoxically, however, as is often, alas, the case, when Danry finally did decide to tell the truth, nobody would believe him any more.

The King himself read the statement and kept it in his pocket for several days. That was the importance so pitiful a case had assumed. Releasing Danry was out of the question, as he was most surely guilty or mad. However, the apothecary's apprentice Binguet, who had shared Danry's room, knew nothing of his neighbour's plans. He was set free, but advised not to utter a word to anyone about the little he knew of the case.

At the Bastille Danry was surrounded by considerations, although he could not leave his cell like the other prisoners, to go to the library or to take an escorted walk along the towers. He did, nevertheless, receive books and was given a pipe and some tobacco. He was also allowed to write. Berryer himself made sure that the prisoner had no need of anything. He complained of loneliness? He was given a cell mate, who had been accused of spying for the King of England. 'All the secret agents of the crowned heads have plenty of spirit,' Danry would later write, 'and I can say that Joseph Abusaglo had a lot of it . . .' The two young men talked far into the night and played mathematical games. Within a few weeks, they were bound by a deep friendship and promised each other that the first to be released would devote all his energy to obtaining the other's freedom.

Had Berryer been overcome with pity for Danry, as the latter liked to believe? Perhaps. But more probably he hoped that enough kindness would induce Danry to reveal what he had obstinately continued to hide since his imprisonment. Indeed, everyone at Court was convinced of the existence of accomplices and perhaps instigators higher up. Why not Maurepas himself, who in that summer of 1749 had been brought to final defeat by the Marquise de Pompadour and forced on the road of exile? So interrogations and reports signed by the lieutenant-general of police piled up. Being also a magistrate, the head of the police force was of the opinion that the investigation was not over and that there was no reason to bring Danry to trial.

That was why after three months of detention at the Bastille, a new *lettre de cachet* ordered the prisoner's transfer to the Castle-keep of Vincennes. In fact, in a letter to the minister, Berryer had stated, 'It appears to me that his freedom is a long way off. In this case, don't you think it advisable to have him transferred to the Castle-keep of Vincennes so that he can make room for us at the castle of the Bastille where we are constantly in need of extra space . . .' Poor Danry. When they came to fetch him without any explanation, he thought he was being released. He embraced his cell mate and swore that he would be faithful to their mutual pledge. He promised that he would do all he could to have him freed too.

3

Escape from Vincennes

The Castle-keep of Vincennes had no cause to envy the Bastille in terms of reputation. This imposing fortress, which also only received prisoners by *lettres de cachet*, operated somewhat as an extension of the Bastille. The sturdy keep had been completed by Charles V, who had made it his residence. Charles VII used it as a country estate in the middle of the forest of Vincennes. Louis VI, a relentless hunter, often went there; but finding the rooms on the various floors of the keep rather uncomfortable, he had a central building put up next to it, which in the reign of Louis XIV, became the King's pavilion. Thus left empty, the keep was used to house prisoners, except in the reign of Henri III, who again made it a place of retreat where he came to hide his royal attacks of religious melancholy.

Initially, the prison was exclusively for noblemen, who came with their dogs and servants and sometimes even with their wives. With the civil wars of the Fronde in the mid-1600s, Vincennes, like the Bastille, was filled to capacity. Lower-ranking prisoners were then allowed to enter, but when Danry passed through its walls one beautiful morning in the summer of 1749, despondent to have thought for an instant that he was being released from the Bastille, he was told that he was being placed there as a favour. The surgeon, who soon came to pay him a visit in a large, quite comfortably furnished cell, tried to explain this to him in order to allay his despair. Only people of noble birth or of the highest distinction were sent there. Besides, at that very moment, two cells further down, was M. Diderot, who had arrived the week before. He was taking advantage of his imprisonment to make corrections to the proofs of his work, the *Encylopédie*. What the surgeon of Vincennes did not go on to say was that the governor had been surprised that 'the Court had been determined to send a subject of this sort to the castle'.

But neither the comfortable cell, located on the top floor of the keep and affording a superb view of the forest of Vincennes and the surrounding countryside, nor the long walk each day in the park, nor the unlimited amount of paper, ink and tobacco could console Danry, who soon fell ill. He suffered from a major hernia, which succeeded in prostrating him. But he would not even allow the surgeon, who had come to take measurements for a bandage, to bleed him. Without losing countenance, the latter replied that as he was not paid for bleeding the prisoners, he would be more than happy to exempt Danry from 'this formality'.

Despite this, Versailles persisted in thinking that Danry was concealing the name of some high-ranking schemer for whom he had only been the agent. The Court's version was that Danry had become scared at the last moment, unless he had hoped for a double reward and had come to Versailles to play the double agent. On 7 October, the King's chief general physician, Dr Quesnay, was sent in person to Vincennes to see Danry, to obtain the much desired revelation. On his return, Quesnay wrote to Berryer: 'I only saw a man in a daze who, despite his state, continued to corroborate what he said in his original statement. But he was so confused that I had difficulty in obtaining more than a few words at a time . . .'

All the same, Danry found enough strength to set pen

to paper again and write the Marquise de Pompadour a sincere, heartbreaking letter:

> Madam, if distress, exacerbated by hunger, was the motive behind my committing an insult against your dear person, it was not at all with the intention of causing you any harm, as God is my witness. If his divine grace could intervene today on my behalf to reveal to you my soul repenting of its great error, and the tears I have shed these past 198 days at the sight of iron bars, you would have pity on me, Madame. In the name of God, who is your light, may your rightful anger be appeased by my repentance, by my misery, by my tears. One day God will reward you for your humanity. Madame, you are almighty. God has given you power over the greatest king on earth, his beloved, he is merciful, he is not cruel, he is a Christian. If his divine power could favour me with obtaining my freedom through your generosity, I would rather die and eat nothing but grass rather than risk it a second time. I have founded all my hopes on your Christian charity; hear my prayers, do not abandon me to my unhappy fate. . . .

The lieutenant-general of police promised that he would personally ensure that the letter was transmitted to Mme de Pompadour. He kept his word, but the petition remained fruitless. Then Danry sank into despair, refusing all food and no longer wanting to get out of bed. In view of this situation which lasted for several days, the governor grew concerned and suggested a transfer to the lunatic asylum at Charenton where there were 'perhaps ways of making unwilling people eat'. Berryer opposed this and called in a doctor he knew, whose talents he had already been able to appreciate in cases of mental illness.

Six days passed and Danry had not eaten a thing. Would he perish from lack of nourishment? Berryer's physician, Dr Herment, arrived on the scene. He did all he could to calm a mind that seemed to him to be greatly troubled. Berryer advised the doctor to say that freedom was close at hand. Yes, he said, the punishment is almost over. Danry listened eagerly and began to take some broth in the kind doctor's presence. He immediately reported back to the lieutenant-general of police.

Six months had gone by since Danry's attempt to let himself wither away. Six months at the end of which he had come to realize that his release was not imminent and that he had been tricked. This was why he was now determined to escape.

It was by observing the comings and goings at the foot of the castle-keep in a small garden set aside for a Jansenist priest also being held prisoner that he began to plan his escape. The degree of freedom enjoyed by the cleric would enable him to get past the sentries. He would pretend to be looking for him and walk across the priest's garden which was directly connected to the area where he took his daily stroll. The only problem would be shaking off the two guards accompanying him. Danry imagined getting them used to the gradual increase in the speed at which he went down the endless number of stairs in the keep, until the day when he would abandon his guards on the spot. A bold, but confusing, plan, it was on the same level as the booby-trap parcel sent fourteen months earlier to the Pompadour.

On 25 June 1750, at two o'clock in the afternoon, taking no time to reflect further on this uncertain plan, Danry darted down the stairs as his guards ushered him out for his walk. The first part of the plan went smoothly, as no one set off the alarm when he hurtled down the stairs four at a time, as he had been in the habit of doing for several weeks already. Once down the stairs, he pretended to knock at the connecting door to begin his false search for the priest. But he did not know that this door had been condemned for some time and that while he struggled in vain, his guards would catch up with him. Then came a miracle in the form of a black spaniel which, clearly lost, began to leap up with prodigious bounds. It jumped up to Danry, barking, and then ran towards the end of the garden where it reared up against the entrance door which opened under its attack. The door had not been locked!

In a second Danry was through the door while the heedless footsteps of his guards could still be heard on the staircase. A sentry was on duty outside. Danry passed very quietly in front of him, performing this new miracle without drawing any attention. Soon he slipped off and began to run across the fields and vineyards until he collapsed with fatigue in the direction of Saint-Denis. It was four o'clock in the afternoon. Birds were in full song in the sunny sky which Danry stared at as he lay on his back in a wheat field, drunk with happiness and emotion. He was to stay like this for more than five hours, waiting for nightfall and feverishly going over his plans again and again.

As evening drew on, Danry made his way to Paris, but avoiding the main road. He spent the night by an aqueduct near the Saint-Denis gate. As dawn broke, he entered Paris and found a room at the Soleil d'Or, an inn on the Rue Neuve-Saint-Denis. For three days he sought out his former acquaintances until he came across a pretty girl named Annette Benoît, whom he had met shortly before his arrest. With his southern gift of the gab, Danry told her that he was being followed and that his life depended on her. He also added that he loved her. How could Annette resist?

First she went to see Binguet, who had his headquarters

in a beer tavern not far from there. But this character had been so frightened by his stay in the Bastille that he did not want to hear any more about his former companion. The same was true for other friends who categorically refused to meet Danry, who at that hour was surely being actively sought by the police. Some even barely agreed to lend or reimburse a few *livres*. As for Annette, she was aware that she risked prison by helping the runaway, but she was elated at the idea of saving him. Better still, she was able to convince several of her female companions to help them. They delivered letters and began to look for safer and less expensive lodgings than the inn. Meanwhile, Danry spent a night underneath the aqueduct at the Pré Saint-Germain. The next day, the girls found him temporary lodgings and he remained there for two days without going out, in the tender company of Annette.

But what was he to do? It was impossible to stay in the same place for more than a night, because there was a risk that these girls, however devoted to his cause, would make some inadvertent remark. He would have to flee and leave the all too heavily policed capital. But where was he to go? And where could he find money? Annette was too poor to give him any. So after much thought, the fugitive told himself that after all he had only committed a peccadillo and that he was quite wrong to behave like a criminal. An honest subject who had received sufficient punishment with fourteen months of prison did not behave like that. Besides, it would surely be appreciated if he took the initiative to show up.

It did not take Danry long to convince himself of this simple line of reasoning, and on 29 June he wrote not one letter, but three: one to Mme de Pompadour from whom he requested favour, the second to Dr Quesnay who had been so kind to him at Vincennes and the third to the lieutenant-general of police to whom he expressed his readiness to follow all his wise advice and even return to Vincennes! In an act of rashness, he wrote his new address on the three letters the better to throw himself on the generosity of his august recipients. He awaited a reply 'c/o M. Chatelet, innkeeper, Rue Saint-Maur, opposite the Hospice des Incurables in the Saint-Germain district'.

Meanwhile, an upheaval was going on in the services of the lieutenant-general of police which would certainly have surprised Danry. Berryer had barely informed the minister of the bad news when the latter went into a fit of rage: 'Nothing is more imperative or urgent', he enjoined, 'than to resort to every imaginable way of trying to catch the prisoner.' All available means were soon put into action. The police even went so far as to print a large number of 'wanted' signs for the fugitive, which were sent to all the constabularies around Paris. A circular was included that read:

> The King's intention is, Sir, that you immediately carry out the most thorough search in your department for the man named Danry and that you arrest him wherever he is hidden. Use all your knowledge and skill to capture this person, and count on a tremendous reward if you succeed. Give a copy of the description I enclose here to every one of your patrolling officers and use the most skilled spies. In a word, do all you can to find him . . .

Such a deployment of force indicated the extent to which Versailles persisted in believing that Danry was keeping the secret of a plot. All the gaolers and guards on duty at the Castle-keep of Vincennes on the day of the escape were locked up in the Bastille. After it had been ascertained that they had not been bribed, they were released after a few months of punishment for their negligence. An amusing anecdote is recounted, that one of these men, Nicolas Vienot, had to be asked, not without some embarrassment, to return the set of keys he had taken with him inadvertently to the Bastille!

They searched for Danry everywhere, but he was nowhere to be found. So, it is possible to imagine the effect Danry's letters had when they arrived, all with his address at the bottom. Annette was arrested twenty-four hours before the never-failing Saint-Marc went to fetch Danry at his inn on 1 July. His escape had lasted a mere five days. Curiously, Annette, who had been a flagrant accomplice and had readily owned up to it, only stayed in the Bastille for two weeks. Those at Versailles took plotters seriously, but love was forgiven. As for Danry, he was not treated so well, despite his pleas. He was taken to the Bastille where he was thrown into a dungeon with his legs shackled. He was to stay there for eighteen months.

4

Prisoner of the Bastille

There were several forms of detention at the Bastille, depending first of all on the seriousness of the offence, but also on the social status one had before entering, which would not be forgotten through imprisonment. Important men locked up at the Bastille benefited from considerable advantages, especially if the offence they had committed was not too serious.

Thus in 1695 the commander of a cavalry section, Charles de Vergeur de la Granche de Courlandon, was found guilty of insubordination and, like all important people, had the privilege of receiving his *lettre de cachet* in person requesting in a very civil manner that he report to the Bastille. It would have been unthinkable to send the letter first to the governor of the prison and to send the arresting officers without any explanation. M. de Courlandon therefore made his appearance one evening in January alone before the drawbridge of the Bastille. The governor himself came to present his excuses. There was no room yet ready for him. M. de Courlandon was kindly requested to spend the night at the King's expense in a near-by inn with the sign reading La Couronne. The next day, at eleven o'clock in the morning, the military commander returned to the Bastille, ate at the governor's table and was finally able to occupy his cell.

Another important individual of this kind arrived at the Bastille in the minister's carriage when Marmontel, managing editor of the French periodical *Mercure de France*, and sentenced to a few days' punishment at the Bastille for impertinence, was allowed time by the lieutenant-general of police to finish printing the last issue of *Mercure* in progress. The lieutenant proposed that they should go to the Bastille in two separate carriages in order to avoid imposing the disgrace of his presence on Marmontel. Marmontel would not have wanted to offend the chief of police and so they went to the Bastille in the same coach. The prisoner's packages and books were hardly searched before being sent up with his servant, who had agreed to accompany him, to a huge room furnished with two beds, two tables, a wardrobe and three cane chairs. Was it cold? The gaoler lit a fire and brought in an ample supply of wood. The mattress was no good and the blankets were dirty. Within minutes everything was changed. Writing materials? Pens, ink and paper were brought on condition that he would have to account for the use of each sheet of paper. The gentlemen were hungry? They were kindly asked to wait in patience.

A moment later, dinner arrived and was served by Marmontel's servant. The meal was quite good and consisted of beans and finely cooked cod in garlic, served in a rather common set of dishes perhaps. There was no dessert, but as Marmontel commented, you had to go without something. His servant, Bury, was about to eat what was left when a knock came at the door. Two gaolers entered with a fine set of china, a white tablecloth, napkins and a sumptuous dinner. Marmontel and Bury realized their mistake and said nothing at first. But, when the gaolers left, they broke out laughing. 'Sir', Bury said, 'you've just eaten my dinner. You'll find it proper if I in turn eat yours.' 'Fair is fair,' Marmontel replied.

Then again there was the son of the head president of the Parliament of Aix-en-Provence, who was imprisoned at the Bastille for debauchery. He shared the governor's table every day, thanks to his pleasant conversation, and stayed there under the pseudonym of Saint-Julien even when there were guests. When large dinner parties were held with important people who might find fault with the governor for this, Saint-Julien was requested, with a thousand apologies, to withdraw to his room, where he was nevertheless brought food from the official table. As for the Marquis de Fresne, he received permission to leave the Bastille, the first time to see his mother, and another time to go to a health spa for his rheumatism, which had got worse because of his stay at the Bastille.

Of course, only a few prisoners benefited from such privileges. But everyone, or almost everyone, could write, receive mail, clothes and provisions if he felt that the food at the Bastille, which was better than average, was insufficient. Many, for example, had their own wine brought in. Everyone could play a musical instrument if he had one, or else read after choosing a maximum of four books from the library's catalogue, which contained books on travel, law, religion . . . Censorship at the Bastille, as elsewhere, was random. Indeed when the lieutenant-general of police, who, among his many duties, was in charge of censuring reading material, took advantage of a book being sent for rebinding (it was entitled *A Poem on God's Greatness* – a subject 'too melancholy for prisoners') to have it removed from the catalogue, the same catalogue was found to contain a *Treatise on Suicide*, which no one thought of striking off the list.

The eight towers of the Bastille all had names. There was Bertodière, Bazinière, Comté ('County'), Trésor ('Treasure'), Chapelle ('Chapel'), Coin ('Corner'), Liberté ('Freedom'), Puys [modern Puits] ('Well'). Each had three to six rooms on top of one another, with one, or sometimes two, prisoners per cell. These rooms were of vast size, and almost all had a large open hearth where a fire was kept burning in the winter. Most of the prisoners could leave their cells once a day to stretch their legs in the inner courtyards or, more rarely, if they were fortunate enough, on the upper platform. But each tower had a dungeon in its foundations, and a garret cell, called a *calotte*, at the top where the conditions of detention were infinitely more severe. The *calottes* were mainly for undisciplined prisoners, whereas the underground dungeons, with or without chains, were used to punish particularly infamous crimes as well as escape attempts.

It was in one of these dungeons that Danry was locked up, with shackles around his ankles. Guilty of escaping, and more suspect than ever of having benefited from outside accomplices and therefore of not having said all there was to say in the booby-trap parcel case, he could not expect the slightest alleviation of treatment, especially since he was only a commoner of the lowest origin and no one, neither family nor friends, enquired after him or came forward to vouch for him. Danry was subject to the severest form of detention; his feet were chained to an enormous pillar and he was forced to lie on a bundle of straw. Twice a day he received a jug of water and a piece of stale bread. Feeble daylight filtered through a narrow chink. The walls sweated with dampness from the near-by moat which let off a disgusting stench, especially at this time of the year when the water level was down. Prostrate, Danry watched the days and nights go by. Every hour was an eternity to him.

But Berryer, informed by the gaolers at the Bastille of this harsh treatment, became concerned. In such cases prisoners had been known to go mad out of despair and solitude. How would he ever discover Danry's secret if such a thing should happen to him? So Berryer arrived one fine morning at the end of autumn 1750 in the underground cell where the prisoner was rotting away. And then the lieutenant of police was surprised at the severity of the regime inflicted on the prisoner. It was obvious that he could not go against orders from Versailles, although he continued to plead his cause, but he could lighten the punishment. If he could not move him out of his dungeon, since the prisoner was under orders to atone for his escape from Vincennes, what could be done for him? Food? Berryer promised Danry that he would again receive the Bastille's normal menu from the next day. Reading and writing materials? Granted.

Danry saw in Berryer a friend and not a policeman. These visible improvements in the miserable conditions of detention, as well as soft exhortations, had rekindled his hopes. Danry had also asked if he could breed small birds whose chirping and liveliness would keep his mind occupied. Permission was granted for this too. But the months continued to go by and with the return of winter, exposing the prisoner to the harsh cold, Danry became increasingly irate instead of being patient. He wrote dozens of letters asking for his surgical instruments which had remained at Vincennes, a dressing-gown, a hat, some breeches, stockings and above all a new cell, considering that there was no air or daylight in the dungeon where he was.

He increased his petitions to the lieutenant-general of police whom he referred to as 'dear Christian', begging him to intervene on his behalf with Mme de Pompadour to whom he wrote likewise: 'Oh God above, grant my prayer, dear Christian lady . . .' The most poignant entreaties increasingly gave way to demands and wrath. Was his 'leaving' Vincennes the reason for his present treatment? As for Minister d'Argenson, who did not see fit

to answer his letters, Danry sent him all the letters of the
alphabet one day, begging him to form from them himself
the words capable of softening his heart. Another day, in
a fit of rage against the Marquise de Pompadour who had
informed Berryer that she would no longer receive his
letters, Danry composed a few vengeful lines in the margin
of a book from the library:

> Sans esprit, et sans agréments,
> Sans être belle ni neuve,
> En France on peut avoir le premier des amants:
> La Pompadour en est la preuve.

> (Lacking in wit, lacking in charm,
> Lacking in beauty and freshness,
> In France it is possible to have the best of lovers:
> The Pompadour is living proof.)

These nasty lines were soon discovered by the gaoler
whose duty it was to examine the library books before they
were lent out again, in order to prevent any clandestine
correspondence. The gaoler passed them on to the governor,
who referred them to the lieutenant of police, who in turn
showed them to the minister. Everyone laughed under his
breath, but at the same time was a bit more convinced that
Danry was really a political enemy of the Marquise de
Pompadour.

Besides, Berryer had not given up hope of obtaining the
name of an instigator from Danry, and why not that of
the former minister Maurepas himself? So he wrote to
Dr Quesnay, one of the distinguished recipients of Danry's
letters: 'It would be a great pleasure to him if you would
pay him a visit. Such a kind act might perhaps induce him
to open up himself to you and truly confess what he has
told me only in part . . .' Quesnay went to the Bastille,
saw Danry in his dungeon and promised him freedom in

exchange for his confession. 'I acted alone, as I've said all along,' cried the prisoner. 'If there really had been a plot, it would have been to my advantage to lay the blame on someone else.'

Another year of imprisonment went by during which the prisoner's mental state deteriorated to such an extent that the lieutenant-general of police abruptly decided upon a transfer to a decent room in the Bastille Puits (Well) Tower, two months before his sentence in the dungeon was up. At the same time, at the King's expense, he provided Danry with a servant to attend to him and especially to keep him company and shake him out of his stupor. All of a sudden, Danry came back to life. The gaolers' silence gave way to the kind ear and soft words of a companion in captivity.

But servants attached to a prisoner could not under any circumstances correspond with the outside world or go back on a decision made of their own free will. Now Danry's servant had a wife and children whom he missed to the point of falling sick. The poor man proved a dismal consolation with his weeping and wailing day and night. Here was Danry, depressed once more and quite ready to share his poor servant's despair. As the remedy turned out worse than the original illness, the servant was released. But so as not to leave Danry alone, he was soon given a new companion, Antoine Allègre. Allègre had been locked up in the Bastille two years earlier for reasons similar to Danry's. He had dreamed up a dark scheme to poison the Marquise de Pompadour involving Minister Maurepas, and the Bishop of Albi and the Bishop of Lodève. To add further weight to the denunciation, which he hoped would earn him a reward, he also sent a forged letter to the favourite's valet, beginning with the words: 'Upon my honour as a gentleman, there are 10,000 crowns for you if

you poison your mistress . . .' But, unfortunately for
Allègre, Saint-Marc was the police officer put in charge of
the investigation, and in that case too he had soon got the
measure of this 'informer whose possible trickery was not
to be overlooked'. As in the case of the booby-trap parcel,
he compared Allègre's handwriting with that of the forged
writing and examined the writing paper. So Allègre was
then arrested by *lettre de cachet,* together with his brother
Jean-Joseph, a monk of the Christian faith, whom Saint-
Marc suspected of complicity. The brother was released
four months later after being found innocent. Nevertheless, the police continued to keep him under discreet
surveillance, because, as the lieutenant-general of police
wrote to Minister d'Argenson, 'He's a live wire and
a hothead who might well be capable of something
interesting.'

Antoine Allègre, who was born in what is today the
Department of Vaucluse, was twenty-four when he arrived
at the Bastille. His parents had originally intended him for
an ecclesiastical career, but he had ended up as head of a
boarding school in Marseilles with the idea that he would
find a position equal to his ambitions, which were very
grand. He was undoubtedly intelligent, had a sharp, original
mind, and his knowledge was already vast, especially in
the sciences, and more particularly in mathematics and
mechanics which he continued to study at the Bastille after
Berryer had books dealing with these subjects specially
purchased for him.

As in Danry's case, there was a motive behind such
leniency. In fact, the Marquise de Pompadour was asking
for new light to be shed on this new affair, and the idea of
putting these two talkative prisoners together might just
reveal some new information on either man. Indeed,
Allègre himself also flooded the lieutenant of police with
memoranda, petitions and even detailed plans for the reform

of industry. Nevertheless, he was initially hostile to any form of cohabitation. 'I beg you, please give me a room to myself,' he wrote to Berryer, 'even if there's no fireplace; I like to be alone, I don't need anyone else, because I know how to keep busy and to plan for the future.'

But it did not take long for the two young men to become as thick as thieves. To such a point that they were soon organizing an underground-mail network, first among the Bastille prisoners and then beyond the prison walls. Messages circulated, but so did money, and even lottery tickets. A loosened stone in the chapel served as a mail box. But it was rare for the hiding places to remain undiscovered by the gaolers for any long period of time. Actually, the guards usually knew nearly all that was happening, and often let the inmates continue solely by order of the lieutenant of police, who by having the messages read to him, was able to acquire a lot of information that he had not already got.

Sometimes practical jokes were played on those participating in the network, and one of the best pranks was that initiated by La Beaumelle. The first time he was locked up at the Bastille was for having falsified an edition of Voltaire's *Age of Louis XIV* in which he had added insulting notes against the d'Orleans family, and the second time was on account of some falsified memoirs of Mme de Maintenon. His inclination for forgery gave him the idea of pretending that he was a woman in his letters to Allègre (although in the minority, there were in fact female prisoners at the Bastille).

Considering the fact that both had a witty mind, the tone gradually became inflamed and Allègre fell madly in love with La Beaumelle, never dreaming that he had found a greater deceiver than himself. The two correspondents had agreed that in case of danger, they would destroy each other's letters. But Allègre was so in love that he could not bring himself to burn the letters from his lover, who was so near and yet so far. A search brought to light the precious package tied up with ribbon and cost Allègre a few weeks in the dungeons, not to mention the sarcastic remarks from the entire Bastille.

But the months and seasons went by, embittering the soul and causing revulsion to the mind. The first to react was Allègre who, sick and fed up with the presence of a guard at his side, seriously wounded him with a knife stab in the stomach, ruining any chance he might have of release. This act earned him several months of solitary confinement, but he would have surely been put on the rack in the Place de Grève if he had been free. Danry was the next to be continually insulting his guards, who found him in possession of an extremely sharp knife – its origin un- known. He again stepped up his letter writing, alternating between threats and pleas. The hellish prolongment of their detention sent both men mad with despair.

'Sir, for the love of God, have pity on me,' Danry wrote in a letter to Berryer. In another to Dr Quesnay, he donated his body. Wasn't he going to die soon? A piece of cloth was sewn onto the letter. Since he had been going through sheer agony for the past fifty-seven months, he reasoned that this little bit of his clothing could not fail to perform miracles. The lieutenant of police, to whom Quesnay transmitted this letter, tersely added: 'A good letter to keep; it conveys some insight into the person's state of mind.'

The letters became increasingly disordered, with compli- cated and ornate handwriting, a fair indication of the imminence of madness. But from time to time Danry returned to a coherent, confident tone, to ask the major of the Bastille for shirts, books or permission to buy tea and fruit salad with his money (which the major continually wondered how he got), because most of the time the food served to him was so bad that all he ate was dry bread. Tired of such an avalanche of letters, the governor of the prison ordered Danry's ink and paper to be confiscated. Alone, since Allègre was in the dungeon, Danry became really desperate. He began to write on a piece of his shirt with his own blood.

Suddenly, at the end of the summer of 1754, after Allègre had been released from his dungeon and put back with Danry in a new room (the fourth in 'the Comté'), the two prisoners' conduct became exemplary. There were no more letters, no more shouting, no more threats. The governor was extremely pleased, but what he did not know was that Danry and Allègre had decided to escape.

5

The Great Escape

Allègre and Danry realized that their release would not be soon in coming, and they even had enough self-conceit to believe that the Marquise de Pompadour was pursuing them with particular hatred. In any case it was certain that no one was examining the many requests in their letters any more, and that their indiscipline could only lead to longer periods of solitary confinement and more generally to a harsher existence at the Bastille. Escape was the only solution to appear now in minds revolted by five years of imprisonment. To want to escape from the Bastille was surely a mad idea, but hadn't madness become a daily companion?

Danry often told his companion the story of his escape from Vincennes, and the two young men had spent entire evenings the previous summer dreaming of escape and freedom. They went over exits and passages hundreds of times. They immediately ruled out the solid double wooden door which was reinforced with impressive iron bars. And even supposing that it were possible to get past the door, they would only get under the feet of an officer or gaoler. As for the single window that let the light into their room, it was rather a chink and would hardly be large enough for a man to squeeze through. Moreover, no fewer than four successive portcullises were fixed in the 6-foot-thick [1.80m.]

wall where the gaolers always first looked when they began their inspection of the cells.

There was of course the huge chimney over the fireplace, checked less frequently, but it also was spiked with metal gratings and bars in several places. And even supposing that it were possible to hoist themselves up to the platform, they would have to contend with an 82-foot [25m.] drop down overhanging a large moat full of water surrounded by another wall on the outside. They would have to find the right tools, make ladders and ropes in silence and conceal everything for months on end. In fact, everything else depended on this last detail. The huge room was sparsely furnished, the trestle beds often searched, and a hiding place seemed impossible.

The two companions went over and over this problem a thousand times. One day, the scientifically minded Allègre came up with a solution. In his previous room, he could hear quite distinctly both the prisoner above him and the one below. In the fourth room in the Comté, where they were, they could only hear the footsteps of the prisoner above them. Yet, on his way back from Mass, Danry had noticed that nevertheless there was a prisoner in the room below. It slowly dawned on Allègre why this was so; their room must have a double floor. On the basis of this hypothesis, Allègre's logical mind soon went into action. Danry followed him with enthusiasm. As the lieutenant-general of police would later say, 'Danry is Allègre's other half.'

One evening, after the gaoler had completed his last round, Danry and Allègre tore two iron pins off the wall which served as a means of support for a folding table which they would obviously leave in its upper position. Two cylindrical lighters were attached to serve as handles. With these home-made tools a tile was removed from the floor and the mortar beneath scraped away bit by bit. At the break of dawn, after an exhausting night's work, the prisoners had to restrain their joy. There was, in fact, quite a large empty space between their floor and the ceiling below. The tile was carefully put back in place and repointed with mortar dust. The sharpest eye would not be able to detect a hiding place there. The real work could now begin.

The task was twofold. They had on the one hand, to prepare the escape route by tearing out the many gratings and bars preventing access to the 30-foot [9m.] chimney, and on the other, to make a rope ladder for the chimney, another of 80 feet [26m.] to get down from the towers, a wooden ladder to get over the outside wall, not to mention all sorts of additional ropes. The two men embarked on nightly activity which was to last for eighteen months. The first rope ladder was made from twisted thread which was obtained by undoing shirts and handkerchiefs thread by thread and transforming them into balls. Luckily, Danry had an extensive wardrobe. But gradually the consumption of linen became enormous. Everything was used: shirts, towels, underpants, stockings, breeches, handkerchiefs . . .

During the winter of 1754–5 the prisoners went around half naked in their cell, constantly demanding more clothes. Danry's request for new shirts was met with a reply from the major of the Bastille, Chevalier, that he already had seven very good ones. But why not give in to a few of the prisoner's whims? The commissioner of the Bastille had two dozen shirts and the same quantity of handkerchiefs made at the King's expense. Major Chevalier did not suspect a thing. Likewise, the linen maid at the Bastille did not seem to notice that the towels and sheets leaving the room of the two accomplices had become smaller, although it was true that the ends had been carefully redone and sewn up again with needles and thread bartered for tobacco through the small-scale contraband trade at the Bastille.

Exhausting work, especially in the chimney, where the

two prisoners took turns at scraping. For hours on end they blew water from their mouths to soften the cement they had marked out. Their hands chafed, they slowly prised loose each grating as they tried to keep their balance on the dangling rope ladder. This demanding task alone would take six months. But once they had gained access to the chimney top, Danry and Allègre were able to go up onto the platforms of the Bastille at night where they found some relaxation from surveillance. They brought back pieces of iron taken from the gun carriages and even a mallet, a drill and some mittens left behind by workers one evening.

They were even careless enough to communicate sometimes with the prisoners in the other towers, the better to satisfy their increasing need for thread. One night, one of the prisoners, who was a mystic, heard voices from heaven. He believed that it was God and the next day announced the great news to his gaoler, who did not fail to report to his superiors that the prisoner's deranged state of mind had worsened.

The long ladder, in turn, took over half a year to make. A huge rope of braided thread had to be transformed into a ladder whose rungs would be reinforced with wooden boards made from fire logs patiently sawn with a home-made saw. The ladder had no less than 151 rungs, each covered with a piece of cloth to avoid any noise from its impact against the wall. Another ladder, which could be taken apart, made of pieces of wood sawn up and assembled, had also to be constructed, along with a safety rope the same length as the long ladder.

But that was not all. Once they had climbed down the towers and crossed the moat and parapet, they would still have to get through the governor's garden, situated on the bastion looking over the Saint-Antoine district, and finally to cross a second moat at the Saint-Antoine gate. This last part of the route was the most dangerous as a guard's round might take the fugitives by surprise. It was decided to avoid that solution and make a hole directly through the wall separating the Bastille moat from the one at the Saint-Antoine gate. But for this, a ferrule would have to be made to enable them to chip away the mortar at the base of the wall and remove the stone blocks.

The prisoners gradually accumulated an impressive amount of material which they stored in the empty space beneath the floor. Each morning, the two accomplices took care to replace the floor tile and to cover up any trace of removal. They did the same with the gratings and bars in the chimney. Since officers and gaolers could enter the cell unannounced at any time of the day, not only did the tools have to be hidden, but also the smallest shavings liable to capture the attention of the visitors. Moreover, the gaolers and policemen liked to creep up quietly to doors and listen to prisoners' conversations. It was true that, exhausted by the nights of hard labour, Danry and Allègre slept during the day, but curiously enough the guards were not surprised by this. For greater security, however, the two men gave code names to all the words concerned with the escape being prepared. The saw was called 'Faun' and the wooden ladder 'Jacob'. The iron bars were referred to as 'Tubalcain' and the rope 'a dove'. As for the empty space beneath the floor, it was called 'Polyphemus', from the cave of the Cyclops . . .

The long ladder was nearing completion when fate once again seemed ready to play one of those dirty tricks whose secret it alone knew. One morning in the month of October 1755 the two prisoners were informed that they were being transferred immediately to another room so that some repairs could be made in their cell. The gaoler did not know if it was the floor or the ceiling that needed the repairs. In any case, they had to hurry to get their belongings together.

Danry and Allègre had difficulty in hiding their horror, but the gaoler attributed this to their usual bad mood . . . For three long months, the two plotters were to be in a state of mortal fear, expecting at any minute to be thrown into a dungeon once their scheme was uncovered. One morning in January 1756 they were moved back to the fourth room in the Comté without a word. They glanced around; the ceiling had been repaired, and the tiled floor was still undisturbed.

In the waking hours of 25 February 1756, on the eve of *jeudi* [now *mardi*] *gras*, Danry and Allègre embraced each other with tears in their eyes. They had just finished their last night of labour in completing the beastly ladder. The great day had arrived. They would attempt to escape that night. It was a perfect time when nights were long and when the river surrounding the Bastille was at its highest level. To wait a day longer would be taking a needless risk.

It seemed as if the day would never end when six thirty finally struck, indicating that dinner would be brought, as it was every evening, by the gaoler Darragon. Darragon had hardly closed the door behind him before the two plotters were feverishly at work. Danry carefully packed two changes of clothing in a leather portmanteau so that he would have clean, dry clothes if the escape was a success. Meanwhile, Allègre removed the long rope ladder from its hiding place and began to assemble the 151 wooden rungs that reinforced it. The wooden ladder was also fitted together. Finally, everything was placed at the foot of the chimney: ladders, ropes, tools, and even a bottle of brandy. Bastille customs were so solidly fixed that a visit after dinner was unthinkable.

It was nearly eight o'clock when the more agile Danry began to climb up the chimney, which he rid for the last time of its metal gratings, chafing his hands once again. For a few long minutes, all the material had to be hoisted up before Allègre could climb to the top with a rope attached at the top. A dark, rainy night shrouded in fog engulfed them. It was a perfect time for an escape. The fugitives climbed down onto the platform where there were no guards keeping watch, while in the direction of the Saint-Antoine district the sound of a fife and drum playing marches was distinctly audible.

The cumbersome rope ladder was carried with difficulty to the neighbouring Trésor Tower, where it was attached to a cannon and then slowly lowered down to the moat. Danry next tied a safety rope controlled by Allègre around his waist, and ventured out first into the immense black space, swinging wildly back and forth over the abyss, but then gradually gaining control in the air and beginning his descent. After what seemed an eternity, he finally reached the moat. His companion immediately sent down the portmanteau, the wooden ladder and the tools and then embarked on the dangerous descent himself. Not far from there, on the parapet of the redoubt on the other side of the moat a guard was on his rounds, completely cutting off access to the governor's garden. The only alternative, as foreseen, was to pierce a hole through the wall separating the Bastille moat from that of the Saint-Antoine gate.

Up to their chests in freezing cold water, the two fugitives began to work on the last obstacle that separated them from freedom. First they made two holes with the drill and then used two iron bars to dislodge the first stone. Their limbs were numb from the cold despite generous gulps of alcohol, their progress was very slow and with terror they saw night drawing on. They had already once had to let a patrol pass overhead. From then on, fearful of being discovered, they kept their ears open and worked even more slowly. The wall was extremely thick and they had already removed several dozen stone blocks, without succeeding in making a hole. Another patrol went by, and the fugitives sank a little deeper in the water. Suddenly, a sentinel stopped directly over their heads. Had they been discovered? A spray of urine came raining down on them, but at the same time gave reassurance.

Dawn was not far off when they finally pierced the wall. They proceeded to enlarge the opening so that it would be wide enough for a human body. Danry went to fetch the portmanteau which had remained at the foot of the Trésor and returned to Allègre who had got through to the other side. Their hearts were already full of joy when a new difficulty arose. The Saint-Antoine moat turned out to be deeper than they had first thought and neither of them could swim. Now they ran the risk of drowning. Luckily, there was a slope on which they could gradually gain foothold and climb to firm ground. When they reached the Chemin de Bercy bordering the Saint-Antoine moat, they fell to their knees to give thanks to God. Then, shivering from the cold, they put on the clothes that had kept dry in the portmanteau. A church bell nearby struck five as they set off resolutely down the main road.

It was nine thirty in the morning when the gaoler of the Comté, Darragon, went up to the two prisoners' room. They were not early risers at the Bastille. Seeing no one in the beds which had not been slept in, he first thought that Danry and Allègre were playing a joke on him and hiding behind the door. But they were not there. Nor were they under the beds. He first examined the window. Not seeing anything abnormal, he then looked up the chimney and saw that the gratings had been removed. He immediately ran to alert the major of the Bastille who was the governor's military adjutant. Still hoping that he would find the

prisoners, he rushed to the platform on the Comté where
he found nothing but the chimney bars scattered about, a
torn sleeve from a dressing-gown and a flat-heeled shoe.
He ran to the parapet and saw the rope ladder hanging
from the Trésor Tower. He rushed down to the moat
where, following other tracks, he discovered the hole in
the moat wall. There was no longer any doubt. The
prisoners had escaped!

A list of the objects Allègre had received from the Bastille
was found on the table in the prisoner's handwriting. On
the second page, he wrote: 'We have not caused any damage
to the Governor's furniture, we only tore up some old
blankets which were of no use to anyone. The others are
intact. If a few towels are found missing, they are near the
water in the big moat where we took them to dry our feet.
– Non nobis, Domine, non nobis, sed nomini tuo da
gloriam! Scito cor nostrum et cognosce semitas nostras.'
[Not unto us, oh Lord, not unto us, but unto thy name
give the glory! Know thou our hearts and understand the
way we take.] Without taking time to decide which part
of the message was humility and which impertinence,
Chevalier ran to the governor's quarters. He had already
been informed of the horrible news. He immediately locked
up the gaoler of the Comté and all the guards who had
been on duty the previous night. There was no doubt that
the escapees had benefited from help outside and perhaps
even within.

Also apprised of the matter, the dismayed lieutenant-
general of police had to inform the minister, and the same
day he sent a commissioner to the Bastille to investigate in
the King's name, with orders to spare no one. For several
days, the guards were questioned at length. They had seen
nothing, and all along they claimed that they had never left
their posts for a second. But the garrison at the Bastille
was made up of invalid soldiers in their fifties and sixties,

and it was more likely that they spent their duty in the warm sentry post than on the wet and windy platforms.

But if they had not seen anything because of the fog, why was it then that they had not heard anything? The guards replied that it was quite impossible because of the carriages riding by until one or two in the morning and because of a fife and drum on the Chemin de Bercy playing marches from ten o'clock at night until one in the morning. In short, it was obviously the garrison's negligence, and not their complicity, that had allowed Allègre and Danry to escape. It remained, however, to be determined how they had been able to obtain ropes and instruments. The mowers who came in the summertime to cut the grass in the Bastille moat fell under suspicion, for they had already been caught bringing letters to the prisoners. At no time whatsoever did anyone suspect that the prisoners could have escaped by their own means.

At the Bastille, in any case, they all found the pill bitter and trembled for their career. The guards were locked up in solitary confinement for several months, whereas the King's lieutenant and adjutant to the governor, D'Abadie, wrote to the lieutenant of police, regarding 'the horrible escape, the details of which will be long and seem bitter', that the disastrous event grieved him tremendously and that all he could say was: 'Mountains, fall on me!'

It had been nearly fifty years since the last escape from the Bastille. It was on 5 May 1709, after 'the famous winter'. The escapee was the Abbot of Bucquoy, prior of Nogent-sur-Seine. He had been accused of smuggling salt and spying for 'M. de Malborough', of acts of impiety and of magic. According to the 'wanted' notice circulated after his escape, he was a hoaxer whose reversible jacket 'hides many things that are not detected when he is searched . . .'

Eight years before, on the night of 30/31 August 1701, Count Boselli had managed to break out, using a rope to

climb down from the top of the towers. The minister at
the time had consoled the governor, who was in total
despair: 'You mustn't take M. Boselli's escape so personally.
It's a most unfortunate mishap, but it's not the first time
such an event has occurred at the Bastille . . .' The minister
was very good, for one practically had to go back to 1465
to find another escapee, Antoine de Chabannes, Charles
VII's faithful follower, who had been disgraced on this
account by Louis XI at the time of his accession. In those
days, people could just walk in and out of the Bastille.
Some accomplices came to visit the Comte de Chabannes,
went for a stroll with him along the platforms and discovered
an unbarred window looking out over the water. What
length of rope would be needed? They asked for string to
catch fish in the moat, got it, and no sooner had the gaoler
turned his back than they began to use it to measure the
distance from the window to the water below. A month
later, the rope, which for reasons of extreme caution had
been manufactured in Rheims, was hidden for a period of
time in the Bastille itself. Then one cold night in March,
Antoine de Chabannes slid down the rope, which he had
tied to the providential window, into a boat where his
friends were waiting.

By the time of the French Revolution, in three and a half
centuries and despite nearly 6,000 imprisonments, the
Bastille would have only seven escapes to its discredit.

The two fugitives' first visit was to one Fraissinet whose
address had been given to them one day by a fellow sufferer
living above them during one of those long shouting
conversations between prisoners in the Bastille through the
chimney flues. The contact immediately turned out to be
fruitful. In the past, it had been part of an underground
network of aid to Protestants fleeing the Cévennes and

Languedoc, but now operating instead as an organization of solidarity between 'regions', like those often formed in Paris at that time where people began flocking from the provinces. Fraissinet took them to Bernard Rouit, a tailor by trade, who lived on the Rue de l'Abbatiale in the enclosure of Saint-Germain-des-Prés. The tailor had agreed to give them lodging without asking the slightest question.

At the end of the month, Allègre was the first to leave for Brussels, disguised as a peasant. No doubt this time the police were at their heels and that to escape abroad was the only chance of not being caught. In the middle of March Danry received a letter from Brussels. Allègre had arrived safely and invited his companion to join him. On the morning of 8 April Danry finally left his host, not without borrowing 48 *livres* he promised on his honour to pay back on his arrival in Brussels. At the Saint-Martin gate, he struck up a conversation with two merchants on their way home to Cambrai, and they decided to travel together on foot at the leisurely pace of 10 leagues [c. 25 miles] a day.

The tiring journey to Cambrai took eight days, whereupon Danry continued to Valenciennes where he planned to take the stage-coach to Brussels. But the national police were searching the stages and an officer asked him where he was going. Most luckily, Danry had had the idea of borrowing Rouit's birth certificate which had on it the town of Digne in Provence. The police officer was delighted, for he too was from Digne. He began to ask Danry what were at first friendly questions, but as Danry's embarrassment grew, the officer's suspicions increased. Suddenly, the officer was urgently summoned to the other side of the square. Danry had come close to being discovered. As for the policeman, he had just missed the best chance of promotion in a lifetime.

At the border, Danry was elated to see the post with the French coat of arms on one side and the Austrian on the other. But his joy was shortlived. When he arrived at the inn indicated by Allègre on the Place de l'Hôtel-de-Ville, he was told that his companion had been arrested three days before.

Allègre had hardly arrived before he was writing an insulting letter to the Marquise de Pompadour, confident that nothing could be done to him in Brussels. Shortly after this, a police-officer from Paris was dispatched with an arrest warrant signed by Prince Charles at the request of the King of France. The matter had been dealt with so quickly that Allègre was already back at the Bastille in a dungeon before Danry had even left Paris. Furthermore, a letter from the tailor, Bernard Rouit, had been found on Allègre. After quick investigation, *lettres de cachet* had sent not only Rouit and Fraissinet to the Bastille, but also the former's mistress and the latter's apprentice, for fear that the little band would alert the fugitive. Another forty-eight hours and Danry would have been caught in his hideout.

Sensing that the innkeepers were obviously burning to go and inform the police of his arrival, Danry said that he would spend the night there. So, he was not clear of prosecution from his torturers, even on foreign soil! He therefore had to go even further away. First, to Holland . . . At nine o'clock in the evening he boarded the Antwerp boat. His French nationality was so obvious that a Savoyard chimney sweep spoke to him in French. Only too happy to find a little friendship, Danry replied and found himself forced to invent a complicated story. What a strange foreigner!

At Rotterdam, Danry who was by now practically penniless, wrote a desperate letter to his mother in which he told her that he was on the run and that he would soon be caught if he did not receive a little money to live on until he was able to find a job. He asked her to send a bill of exchange immediately to 'M. d'Aubrespy, at the poste restante in Amsterdam'. But the fugitive did not know that Saint-Marc had once again been sent on his trail. During his interrogation, the faithful Allègre had wanted to protect his companion by saying that on the eve of his arrest he was preparing to leave for the new Lisbon, then being re-built after the major earthquake a year earlier. Danry would already be there with a small job.

But Saint-Marc found it difficult to imagine Danry in Lisbon while Allègre was in Brussels. He preferred to wait for a clue to turn up to put him on a serious trail. He had Danry's mother's mail intercepted just in case. Once again, his clear-sightedness paid off when the letter from Holland arrived in Montagnac.

The United Provinces valued their independence and their liberties, and an all-out diplomatic procedure had to be put into motion by the ambassador of France on behalf of the King. Danry was portrayed as a dangerous agitator, a sworn enemy of all regimes. The request was favourably received, provided however that the Dutch police force could be in charge of the operations. As for Saint-Marc, he would have to remain behind the scenes, even if he were to come and conduct the investigation himself. The ambassador of France sent a letter of thanks to the municipality of Amsterdam which had finally granted the extradition, stressing that the King had taken the matter greatly to heart. It was an affair of state.

Saint-Marc was sent out disguised as an Armenian merchant to sniff out the trail left by Danry in Brussels. There, the couple who kept the inn bewailed the fact that they had certainly missed a fine reward. Yes, a strangely dressed young man had appeared at their inn, asking to see the Frenchman who had been arrested a few weeks back. They had even gone to warn the police, and after a vague search, they had concluded that the wanted person had left the country. What was the easiest way of leaving the country? asked Saint-Marc. He was told: Take the Antwerp boat and go to any country from there.

Saint-Marc kept an eye on the Antwerp boat, asked questions on various pretexts and visited all the places where French adventurers and refugees were known to go. A Savoyard living in a miserable attic room informed him that a Frenchman who had seemed very worried and had no baggage had transferred from the Antwerp boat to the one headed for Rotterdam on 17 April. He remembered the day very well, for he was returning to Brussels after sweeping several chimneys. He had even spoken to him and found him a bit cracked in the head. The 17th of April was the precise date on which the mysterious visitor had shown up at the inn where Allègre had been arrested. Saint-Marc was ecstatic. The poste restante in Amsterdam was not, like new Lisbon, a false trail intended to mislead the police. Danry would not escape him any longer.

The rest was a matter of routine. Saint-Marc asked his Dutch colleagues to keep an eye on the poste restante, while he, still dressed as an Armenian merchant, began to gather information about Frenchmen recently arrived in Amsterdam. Still under the leadership of the diabolical Saint-Marc, the Amsterdam police tailed a young man two days later who asked at the poste restante if there was a letter for M. d'Aubrespy. He led the police straight to Danry who had managed to find lodgings with one of the townspeople and had therefore been difficult to locate.

The arrest was carried out on 1 June, with a discreet imprisonment in the Town Hall prison, while Saint-Marc remained in the background to avoid any untoward publicity. However, with his usual false modesty, he briefly informed the French ambassador, who immediately dispatched a special courier to Paris. Both at Versailles and at the Bastille there was great rejoicing. 'I hasten to announce the good news to you,' the chief assistant of the lieutenant of police wrote to the major of the Bastille. 'Inform the Governor immediately: Danry, arrested in Holland, is in prison, and you will have him very shortly. The reputation of the Bastille will be saved . . .' The letter ended, 'The news from Holland is that Saint-Marc is regarded as a real magician.'

On 15 June 1756 Danry was returned to the Bastille after three and a half months of uncertain freedom. He was immediately thrown into the dungeon and put in irons. He had a straw pallet and was fed stale bread and water. His case was serious. Escape from a state prison could be punished by death. Even in England, the land of habeas corpus, escapees were punished with the utmost rigour. As for the Baron de Trenck, imprisoned by Frederick II of Prussia, though sentenced to a single year in prison, he had been recaptured after his second escape attempt, and chained up in a dungeon for life. His grave had been dug at his feet with a plaque on which his name was already inscribed.

6

A Difficult Prisoner

Whereas the guards who had kept such a poor watch over him were released, Danry was placed in a dungeon for a long period, perhaps for life. Shackled in irons and lying on a bed of filthy straw crawling with vermin in those summer months, he only received the light of day through a tiny chink high up, which looked out on the inner courtyard. The weeks and months passed, while Danry, who was plunged into the depths of despair, was slowly engulfed in a deep state of apathy. Indifferent to everything, he soon became accustomed to the perpetual silence to which he had been condemned by his gaolers, concerned now with applying the rules and regulations to the letter.

His silence and immobility were such that the rats grew confident and gradually began to roam around his cell. Curiously enough, it was through these creatures that Danry resumed a little interest in life. One rat, fatter than the others, began to accept that Danry was throwing it bread. After several weeks, the rat was tamed, and soon an entire family was sharing the prisoner's meagre meal. Danry was moved to tears of joy. Since he was dead to his own kind, at least the rat population had become his family.

Each rat had its own name. Some roamed about freely and all of them participated in wild dancing parties, which for Danry were times of sheer happiness. In short, the prisoner was returning to life, in spite of his chains and the hard regime of solitary confinement. Later, despite his fetters, he used a piece of elder binding from the fresh bale of straw just brought to him to make a flageolet. As time went on, Danry even tried to tame the spiders in his cell, which were very fat, but he was unsuccessful because these creatures were less easy to deal with than the family of rats.

But the most formidable and most difficult to approach was without question the human species. Nevertheless, Danry thought he would try again and ask for permission to write. Always on the watch for some new revelation, the new lieutenant of police, Bertin, accepted, also deciding at the beginning of the winter of 1756, to ease up on the prisoner's harsh regime by putting him back on the normal Bastille diet. Danry also received a blanket and was allowed to decide whether he wanted the shackles to be taken off his wrists or ankles. (He opted for the latter.)

Despite the fetters still on his wrists and the terrible cold Danry wrote tirelessly, blotting hundreds of sheets of paper. He first wrote on the subject of large-scale state projects which he had been evolving in his mind for a long time. Now, at the Bastille there was a tradition of never scorning this type of literature, or indeed of 'revelations' of hidden treasure, in case, however slight the possibility, the Crown might derive some benefit. Hence, it was not uncommon to see one of the King's engineers in the Bastille courtyard testing some mechanical or chemical experiment under the anguished direction of its promoter.

Danry first proposed a project for the battlefield whereby all senior and junior officers would be equipped with flintlock muskets instead of the outdated halberds still in use, or rather, not in use. The army would be strengthened in this manner by some 25,000 fusiliers who would be even more effective because they were soldiers with many years of experience, who had taken part in innumerable battles.

A second military project aimed at reinforcing the advancement of a column, while other memoranda, 'intended to bring happiness to the people' examined ways of restoring the kingdom's shaky finances: a large supply of granaries in case of famine, financed through taxes levied on marriage licences and embellished with lotteries; an increase in postage duties; various toll fees; and even a rental fee for pews in parish churches. ('It seems', Danry wrote, 'that it would be easier to extract 100,000 souls from purgatory than to raise 100,000 *livres* from the hiring of parish pews.') All with an abundance of detail, a flood of sentences, illustrated with drawings and accompanied by historical references from every age and every country.

Danry recopied each memorandum several times before bombarding all kinds of recipients with them, attempting at the same time to interest his gaolers in the dissemination of so rich an outpouring. Unfortunately for him, the memoranda were read only by the lieutenant-general of police, who did not follow them up. But Danry convinced himself that his proposals had been taken up and carried out and threw himself into calculating how much he had earned the Royal Treasury, surprised that the hundreds of thousands of *livres* he added so generously did not bring him any compensation, and, why not his freedom?

The projects were then followed by letters – an avalanche of letters to the King, to the Marquise de Pompadour, to ministers, to the lieutenant of police . . . Letters of entreaty and despair: 'Lions and tigers run to the rescue at the slightest cry of pain from their own kind. Shall I not find such compassion today among men?' Or again: 'I'm a man, and I've been suffering for eleven years. There is nothing more cruel than uncertainty.' A theme Danry sometimes took up by way of a demand: 'The emperors whom we call barbarians have handed down laws in favour of criminals so that they might have the time to justify and defend themselves.' Let him therefore appear before a tribunal. 'My suffering is not without remedy: I have had no sentence pronounced against me.' He was an innocent, honest man and asked only for permission to justify himself.

In November 1759 a new lieutenant-general of police was appointed. His name was Antoine Raymond Jean Gualbert Gabriel de Sartine, and he was soon to become as famous as d'Argenson in a position he would hold for fifteen years, with enough time to bring about thoroughgoing reforms in the police force. He was only thirty years old when he took over as chief of police but serious in appearance. Moreover, a fine sceptic, with a friendly character and gracious manners, he was entirely of the brand of great intelligent and capable state agents who left their mark so forcefully on the second half of the eighteenth century.

Like them, Sartine continually favoured the spirit rather than the letter, bringing the Paris police force to a level of efficiency unparalleled until then, to such an extent that Catherine II of Russia asked Sartine to send her a report on the Paris police for the better instruction of her own police. As Beaumarchais, an expert on the matter because of his own encounters with the censors, was to say: 'All the affairs of state begin by being told to M. Sartine, the capital's judge and justice of the peace.'

Sartine was interested in everything and everyone, with his network of inspectors, spies, prostitutes and petty criminals weaving a huge spider's web over the souls and bodies of the capital. Sartine was watching inside dubious inns and alcoves, compiling a real *Who's Who* of debauchery in Paris and at Court (such as 'the Prince de Hénin is forgetting his wife. His wife is forgetting him with the Chevalier de Coigny . . .').

Sartine kept a close watch over his prisoners at the Bastille, Vincennes, the large institutions of the General Hospital and the many convents converted into detention centres, such as Saint-Lazare for men and the Madeleine for women. Danry, glorified by his reputation as an escapee from the Bastille and still suspected of not having told everything there was to tell about the plot against the Marquise de Pompadour, therefore interested him. This was why, only a few weeks after his nomination, the police chief took advantage of the Seine's overflowing and flooding part of the prisoner's cell and the gaoler complaining that he had to walk through a foot of water to bring the prisoner his rations, to have him removed from the dungeon and put in a decent room, which did not, however, have a fireplace.

Danry was taken from his underground cell, blinded by the light, his clothes in rags and with a 10-inch beard. He was a sorry sight. He trod heavily, the irons still on his wrists rattling as he walked. At thirty-four, after eleven years in prison, his features marked by harsh confinement in the dungeon, with little hair, he was certainly no longer the fascinating young man whom the pretty working girls in the Saint-Denis district had been pleased to hide after his first escape from Vincennes.

Sartine watched the scene a few steps away. He saw tears rolling down the prisoner's emaciated face. Overcome with pity, he ordered the chains to be removed immediately, and that Danry should be shaved and bathed before being sent to his new cell. The next day, he came there to see him and lavished kind words upon him. 'Your fate is in your hands,' he told him. 'The better your conduct, the easier it will be for me to intervene on your behalf for your release.' Sartine promised that he would soon return and granted the extraordinary favour of reinstating a daily walk on the Bastille towers for the man who, a few years back, had nevertheless escaped that way.

The governor of the Bastille gave in, but nonetheless had

not forgotten the shame inflicted on him and the entire staff at the Bastille by the escape of 25 February 1756. That was why, without informing the lieutenant of police, he chose a cell in the Comté tower whose gaoler was still Darragon, who also had not forgotten.

Danry had again resumed his relentless epistolary activity, not even noticing the months go by. In the summer of 1762 he sent a long 96-page memorandum to the Marquise de Pompadour in which he alternated between pleas and threats. In other letters he begged her not only to grant his release, but also to pay 60,000 *livres* in compensation. Another time, having exhausted all arguments, he wrote: 'Madame, be a woman . . .'

Danry was even more assiduous in writing to Sartine in whom he rightly saw compassion and support: 'Only a person with no heart would not be moved, not only by the long duration of my misery, but also by the state in which I find myself . . . You who have a heart, Sir, I await your compassion . . .' Danry often called Sartine as a witness to the Pompadour's cruelty: 'Is the Marquise de Pompadour a monster in human form? Is her heart as hard as that of the implacable shrew?' Despite his leniency, Sartine grew angry: 'Tell Danry that I for my part refuse to listen to him when he writes to me in that tone.' 'You always have to end up with strongly worded letters,' Danry explained by way of apology.

Danry missed the happy company of his rats and began to breed pigeons between two of his literary efforts. Among the many that flew from chink to chink, he had managed to capture a male with a net he had made of thread from a shirt and sheet – a technique he already knew very well. A female was caught in turn. A nest was built. Baby birds were born. Once again Danry's heart warmed at the sight of the little cooing family.

The prisoner even wanted to send a pair of these pigeons

to the Marquise de Pompadour and became upset when
told that it was impossible. Surprised by his talent, the
officers at the Bastille came to admire the touching picture.
But Darragon was watching all this. Wasn't it the prelude
to a new escape plan? Soon the officers, who only yesterday
were admiring the pigeon-breeding became convinced that
this great happiness had something suspicious about it. One
morning, a triumphant Darragon came in to confiscate the
pigeons.

As a result, Danry grew bitter again, and lashed out at
the lieutenant of police: 'He whose only crime is to have
been born is old enough to die. You, who have already
reached middle age, should not forget that death can take
you by surprise or that fortune can turn her back on you,
as she has done with many a great man. Need I remind
you of M. le Comte de Maurepas, who was the King's
favourite? If such an unfortunate event should befall you
today, what good could I say of you? . . . I beg you to
grant me a short interview and some paper.' When Sartine
did not answer quickly enough, Danry proceeded to insults:
'And you, Sartine, you barbarian, heart of stone!'

Sartine did not pass on the letters addressed to the
Marquise de Pompadour or the ministers, as he believed,
rightly, that they would work against Danry's interests. As
for those he received personally, sometimes in whole
packets, he tried to reduce the flow by giving strict
instructions to the major of the Bastille: 'If Danry wants to
write me again, tell him that he is excused from doing so
and that I exonerate him from this task.' However, Danry
did not feel that he was exonerated and continued to write,
the more since he received no replies and suspected that his
letters were being kept at the Bastille. So, despite the
inalienable right of the King's prisoners to write to the
authorities, it was decided to deprive Danry of ink and
paper, especially since the major suspected him of keeping

up a secret correspondence with the other prisoners.

But Danry was not to be silenced in this way. To compensate for the lack of paper, he crumbled up bread in his hands, mixed it with saliva and flattened it to make tablets the size of a page of a notebook. Instead of a pen, he used a fishbone (from a carp) which he split in two. All he needed now was ink. His blood would once again do the trick. He tied up a finger tightly and after a few minutes, when the finger tip had become congested, he pricked it with another fishbone and carefully collected some drops of blood which he mixed with a little water in the bottom of a mug.

There was great agitation at the Bastille when a first packet of these letters arrived on the governor's desk. It was understood that it was not enough to punish such determination with a renewed period in the dungeon where Danry would only resume some other new enterprise. Better this time to try persuasion, by sending the infernal prisoner the Bastille confessor, who was a Jesuit highly skilled in the art of penetrating minds and souls.

Furthermore, Father Griffet was not just anyone. Both theologian and historian, he taught literature at the Louis-le-Grand school and had been preacher to Louis XV. He arrived one fine morning in Danry's cell, showed interest in his schemes and asked a multitude of questions about his past life and his escapes. Flattered by this interest, Danry readily talked, although he was surprised that the preacher did not want to hear his confession. There was no question of that! Imperceptibly, they came to the matter of the tablets written with Danry's blood. Father Griffet expressed his horror: wasn't that a step in the direction of suicide? Did the prisoner no longer believe in God? Yes, of course he did. But the Jesuit also expressed his admiration: If Danry had had Cardinal de Richelieu or the King of Prussia as his masters, they would certainly have used his genius instead of suppressing it in the depths of a dungeon.

Before leaving the cell, Father Griffet promised that Danry would once again be provided with ink and paper in exchange for his promise never to write with his blood again. Sartine gave approval to this compromise, considering that, after all, Danry's epistolary activity would help him to be patient. So the prisoner was given everything he asked for: quill pens, large quantities of ink, 'Tellière' paper, whose large format and rough grain met with the incorrigible scribe's approval.

The letters resumed, more than ever. 'He writes like a madman,' the major of the Bastille, Chevalier, said in distress. And indeed, as the months went by, Danry began to go mad with despair. 'You tell me to keep calm,' he wrote to Sartine, 'keep calm . . . How do you expect me to keep calm?'

In the Bastille, the staff tried to make life as comfortable as possible for the prisoner and to help him bear more patiently the loss of the best years of his life. When he complained of the monotonous food, he received more varied meals. More generally, his requests for clothes and supplies were met. Danry shamelessly took advantage of the situation, asking, for example, at the same time, for two flannel cardigans from England ('for my rheumatism,' he said), two silk kerchiefs for his neck, a pair of stockings, a snuffbox lined with cardboard, a small spyglass (which he requested as 'a small favour' from M. Sartine).

Everything arrived ten days later, except for the spyglass. The lieutenant-general of police apologized, but it was not customary to provide prisoners with telescopes. To compensate, the lieutenant of police, who was responsible for the police force and the provision of supplies to a city like Paris, took the time to enquire personally from Chevalier what had become of a trunk, a portmanteau and a pair of boots Danry had been asking for.

One winter, Danry wanted a pair of fur-lined gloves. He was given several pairs from which to choose. Did he want slippers too? His feet were measured and the cobbler was ordered to make a pair of shoes at the same time. It was all delivered, still at the King's expense, together with two pairs of woollen undersocks and a winter cap. Far from considering himself satisfied, Danry continually wanted more things. He was only refused a grammar book and a dictionary, since it was felt that he wrote well enough as it was.

Danry insisted and became angry, but the major told him that he would not pass on this request, even if Danry were his own father. In revenge, Danry refused a pair of breeches which had just been made for him. The distressed major of the Bastille reported the incident to the lieutenant of police: 'This prisoner is stubborn and has refused to date to accept the fine pair of breeches that M. Rougemont has had made for him. They have an excellent lining, silk garters and are in the very best condition . . .'

And in fact Danry became increasingly unruly. He continually asked to see a surgeon, a physician or an oculist, complaining of all sorts of illnesses of which the least serious was rheumatism contracted in the Bastille dungeons. On fast days he wanted fish under the pretext that he did not eat eggs, artichokes or spinach. On feast days, he swore like the devil because his poultry had not been cooked in fat. Since he was an important prisoner, he should be treated as an important prisoner and not like a common man of the kind sent to Bicêtre. There are some things that should never be said . . .

Commissioner de Rochebrune, who was responsible for the prisoners' supplies, did not know how to please Danry: 'You entrusted me', he wrote to the major, 'with the task of having a dressing-gown made for M. Danry, who wants it of blue *calmande* fabric with red stripes. I have had it

requested at twelve different shops and not one of them
has any at all and would never want to, because nobody
would buy this kind of *calmande*, they said. I don't see why
we should cater for the outlandish tastes of a prisoner who
should be content with a warm, comfortable dressing-
gown.' On another occasion, Danry refused four kerchiefs,
saying that they were fit for galley-slaves. He wanted six
large blue-coloured printed cotton ones and two muslin
cravats. If there was not enough money in the royal treasury,
he added, they should ask the Marquise de Pompadour.

Allègre was also giving his guards a rough time. Released
from solitary confinement much later than Danry, he was
rightly considered the brain behind the escape of 1756 which
everyone at the Bastille recalled with bitterness. He was
also kept under close watch and systematically refused what
Danry obtained so easily. He had no fire, light, bed sheets,
table linen, paper or ink. 'He put all those things to bad
use in the past,' the adjutant to the governor explained to
Sartine, 'and I suppose he'd have the same designs if he
had the same means, which I beg you to refuse him.'

Allègre still found the means to write in his detention
room, not with his own blood, but on the tin dishes and
plates. To punish him, he was served his food on earthenware
dishes. Yet he wanted to present projects to the King, and
as he was readily considered an inventive genius, he was
carefully given what he needed to prepare a study on Greek
fire which it was promised would be sent to Versailles.

Sartine found the man intelligent and took an interest in
his writings. Could his detention not be lightened somewhat?
The reaction from the staff at the Bastille was immediate.
'Beware,' the major warned. 'This is a man who cuts off
a little from his clothes lengthwise one week and a little off
crosswise another week. He then does the same with sheets

and at the end of the year he has enough thread to make a rope and escape.' In other words, he was an incorrigible and very dangerous individual, who always had some new trick up his sleeve.

Allègre confirmed his guards' fears by behaving in an increasingly violent manner. They would continue to serve his food in earthenware dishes? He broke them. They refused him sheets? One day when he was angry, he threw all his bedding out of the window and his clothes and underwear as well. They stopped giving him wine and in the end were so fed up that they chained him up again. But his outbursts of anger continued and soon the prison authorities wondered whether he was feigning insanity or whether he really was insane. 'This prisoner would try the patience of a saint,' the major of the Bastille commented to Sartine.

In June 1764 no day went by without Allègre breaking something. Nothing could resist his cold anger, neither the furniture nor the windows. The guards feared him and would not go near him. A doctor took the risk of visiting him. Had he a pain anywhere? 'No, I'm quite happy', Allègre replied in a toneless voice as he walked barefoot over pieces of glass from the window he had broken once again. His guards' anger turned to pity. It was a tragedy to end up in such a state. Once again, too long a period of detention had driven a prisoner mad.

On the night of 7/8 July 1764, Allègre was transferred to the lunatic asylum at Charenton. Extraordinary precautions were taken after it had been explained to the four escorts from Charenton that the prisoner was no less than the kingpin of escape. 'He can do just with his fingers,' the major of the Bastille added, 'what anyone else couldn't do with all kinds of tools.' On the stroke of midnight, a tightly chained Allègre was hoisted into a carriage. Along the way, as he asked where he was being taken, one of the escorts told him that he was being taken to an ordinary house near Paris where he would be better off. At this he spoke very calmly about his childhood, his arrest, his escape from the Bastille. 'I'm not at all mad,' he added. When he arrived at Charenton, he was put in a cage for raving madmen. After a while, Allègre complained that he would have had a better time staying where he was.

The authorities also began to wonder if Danry was not also mad. 'The incorrigible Danry is up to his devilish tricks again,' Chevalier complained. A series of angry outbursts began, and when 'Allègre's other half' was not insulting his guards, he was stirring up prisoners entering, and also departing from, the Bastille, proclaiming his innocence in stentorian tones. Now, there were as many prisoners leaving as there were new ones arriving (the one explaining the other) – which caused the Bastille staff to fear that the newly freed prisoners would spread word in the capital of the complaints from a man they found was becoming such a nuisance. There were plans to transfer him to Mont-Saint-Michel or the Château de Roanne – in any case to an isolated detention centre far from agitators in the capital.

But in contrast to his other half, Danry was able to enjoy periods of calm before too severe a punishment was inflicted. So he resumed his tireless epistolary activity. 'I'd wager my head against 5 *sols* that you don't think about me more than you think about Muhammad's camel,' he wrote to Dr Quesnay on 30 June, 1762. 'You don't fulfil the duty of an honest man by forgetting me in this horrible prison where you've put me.' (Danry felt, in fact with some degree of reason, that it was Quesnay's connections at Versailles that were the cause of the prolongation of his detention.)

Only once did Danry receive a letter from his mother: 'Please don't do me the injustice of believing that I have forgotten you my dear, fond son . . . You are all I ever think of. You fill my every thought . . .. Your misfortunes will some day be over and perhaps that day is not far off . . .' Indeed, the woman who signed herself 'Widow Daubrespi', also sent a moving plea to the Marquise de Pompadour, but she thought it wise not to tell her son this. It was a wise precaution, since her request remained without effect. Likewise, the heartbreaking reply that the prisoner in the Bastille wrote to his mother was not delivered.

Once and for all, it was decided that his letters would be kept in the Bastille where from then on entire packets piled up. Periodically the major of the Bastille would give a batch of them to Sartine. 'This lot', he said one day, 'is filled with abuse, nonsense, misery. I believe that the prisoner is filled with gall and bitterness. It's venom in its purest form.' His room was searched periodically always with the discovery of new letters, vituperative memoranda copied over and over again, not to mention a supply of paper of mysterious origin. Everything was confiscated, and Danry was deprived of his daily walk for a month, because he would not say where he had obtained the paper, stating that he had had it 'for ages'.

And the cycle would start all over again, with new letters expressing his despair: 'I've been suffering now for a hundred thousand hours', one of them read. 'I can't take it any more, I can't take it, I'm cracking up,' another one read. In February 1763 the Bastille cannons had been fired for several days in celebration of the Treaty of Paris which called an end to the Seven Years War. 'I'm not jealous to hear everyone laughing and shouting with joy,' Danry commented, 'but I'm tired of suffering; I can't take it any more . . .'

Sometimes the form was risky, as when he wrote to the lieutenant of police: 'Listen to the voice of justice deep

down within you.' But what did the form matter, when
the poor prisoner was in the process of going mad with
despair. 'When Danry writes like this,' Sartine reported to
the minister, 'it's not that he's mad, but in despair from
his imprisonment.'

Despite the sporadic threats and punishments that he had
inflicted upon Danry for his escapades, Sartine finally had
pity on this oldest inhabitant of the Bastille. In fact, most
prisoners did not stay very long in the Bastille, with the
duration of detention usually ranging from a few months
to a year, more rarely two years. Only a tiny minority
were still there beyond five years. That meant that by now
Danry had beaten the record with fourteen years of
imprisonment.

At the end of August 1763, during one of his trips to
Versailles, Sartine tried to plead with the minister for
Danry's release. Could he not at least be transferred to the
new colony being set up on the island of La Désirade,
where many other bad cases were sent? He was told
categorically that this fellow had to stay at the Bastille and
be patient.

7

The Year the Marquise de Pompadour Died

When the lieutenant of police informed Danry, in carefully chosen words, of the failure of his application, the latter decided, with one of those sudden changes that were his speciality, to count no longer on anyone but himself to regain his freedom. Thus, he changed his attitude overnight, no longer causing scenes or even badgering his guards to get some new petition passed to Mme de Pompadour. 'Talk of my release is just about as frequent as talk of abolishing taxation and capitation,' Danry sighed in an apparently resigned tone to Major Chevalier, who had come to pay him a visit.

Thus began a spate of medical problems. Danry complained of the infirmities overtaking him. He was gradually losing his sight. His hernia was worsening and his rheumatism was totally crippling him because of the years spent in the dungeon. Now that the prisoner had ceased to shout or to insult anyone, they wanted nothing more than to treat him kindly, gladly sending physician, surgeon and oculist to him. In addition to these remedies, Danry was chiefly rewarded under orders from the Faculty, by the resumption of his walks on top of the towers which had been denied him and replaced by a short stroll in the inner courtyard. This was precisely the result he was counting on.

He still had to find a passer-by who looked sufficiently

trustworthy to send a message. From the top of the platform, Danry had a clear view of the apartments in the buildings surrounding the Bastille and understood by now that it was there that he had to direct his efforts rather than on the passers-by. Patiently, he concentrated on observing all the occupants he could see there. He was especially on the lookout for women whose kindness and tenderness of heart, he thought, would be more susceptible to pity. Hadn't he already been able to move Anne the Benoît with the recital of his misfortunes after his escape from Vincennes?

He soon noticed two young women working alone in a room, whose features looked gentle and pretty. At first Danry was not able to attract their attention. The two working girls often looked down to see what was happening in the street, but did not think to raise their eyes. And then one morning, when Danry's daily walk was almost over, one of the girls saw him beckoning to her. They waved to each other. Contact had finally been made.

They were two little laundresses, Lebrun by name, the daughters of a wigmaker in the neighbourhood. There were so many dark legends in circulation about the Bastille that this prisoner who had waved to them with such gentle reserve already excited their compassion and curiosity to the highest degree. From the next day they were already keeping watch on the place where the prisoner had appeared to them. When he finally appeared, they were ecstatic. My God, what an event in their life! He was surely some very important person locked up there for reasons certainly unjust, perhaps for a love affair. Furthermore, seen from afar, Danry still looked handsome, although he was approaching forty and his features were becoming heavier. But all the same, this person was very interesting.

Danry sensed all this. Had he been free, he was a man who would have undoubtedly achieved success through women. But the problem was that he had got off to a wrong start with number one, the Marquise de Pompadour. Now, in any case, he was trying to make the girls understand by complicated signs that he wanted to give them a message and that they had to go down to the street to receive it. Of course, the two sillies finally consented. So a first message was thrown over the wall in a weighted bag that the industrious prisoner had made from the lining of a pair of leather breeches. The note told the adventurous story of his youth and his misfortunes. In any case he was very wealthy and he offered half of his riches to the girls. But was that really necessary to obtain their devotion?

From then on, during the winter of 1763/4, a real courier network was organized. There were letters for great writers and other famous people which the author hoped would not fail to arouse public opinion; a new memorandum of the greatest length against the Marquise de Pompadour in which 'her birth and her disgrace, all her thefts, her cruel acts, were exposed'; new versions of military projects to be transmitted to top engineers after the devoted young women had recopied them.

Every time a new message was transmitted, Danry was informed by an agreed signal in the form of a large black cross on the wall of the building. But soon he began to run out of ink, and the industrious prisoner did not want to draw attention to himself by asking for more. So he managed to make some of his own by mixing black soot and oil from one of his medicines.

At the end of winter, however, Danry made a silly mistake which cost him a month of being deprived of his daily walk, thus interrupting his correspondence. One morning, it had snowed. The platform of the Bastille was covered by a spotless thick blanket. The prisoner had immediately begun to throw snowballs at his guard, but the guard did not want to play. So Danry had found that it was more amusing to throw snow at the heads of the passers-by. Danry was having so much fun that his gaoler, instead of intervening, had thrown some too. Unfortunately, an officer had seen them from the inner courtyard, requesting and obtaining punishment for the prisoner and his guard.

'My snowballs, ridiculous stuff . . .', Danry had stated in defence, thinking that it would not be a sufficient motive to deprive him of his daily walk. As for the major, who was always one step behind a plot, he suspected that Danry had attempted to make contact with someone on the outside.

On 16 April 1764, at 9.15 in the morning, Danry who had resumed his cherished walk along the towers, rushed to greet his two accomplices. They had barely seen him than they began to betray the utmost excitement, waving to him frantically. What was going on? The two girls then unrolled a large sheet of paper on which could be read distinctly the words: THE MARQUISE DE POMPADOUR DIED YESTERDAY.

Danry was overwhelmed with joy. Since the woman whom he had had the complacency to consider his personal enemy was dead, nothing and no one could now challenge his freedom. No sooner back in his cell, Danry set about packing his trunk, expecting at any minute that someone would come to inform him of the time of his release. But the day went on and nothing happened. And nothing on the following days either.

So a furious Danry wrote to Sartine, to request that he come to see him concerning the matter known to him. Intrigued, the lieutenant of police wasted no time. 'Sir,' Danry said to him, 'since the Pompadour is dead, what is the delay in releasing me?' Sartine was dumbfounded. No sooner had he heard of the Pompadour's death, than he had gone to the Bastille to inform the officers personally with the strictest orders to keep quiet about the death before the prisoners. Now, if there was a prisoner in the Bastille who was to be kept in the dark it was surely Danry. How had he found out? Danry, who said that it was public rumour, only made his case worse. There was no public rumour. Who had informed Danry? His confession was the price of his freedom. He did not want to reply? He would be thrown into a dungeon, on bread and water.

But Sartine was certainly not a bad man and although he remained obsessed by the mystery of how Danry had found out about Mme de Pompadour's death, he was of the opinion that after fifteen years of imprisonment for a miserable affair, the time had come to free the prisoner at the risk of exiling him, if need be, from France, or at least in the mountains of the Languedoc. Thus would justice be done and so would everyone be at peace. He had Danry removed from the dungeon after a month and came to visit him in person. 'Let's not talk about the past anymore,' Sartine said. The first day I go to Versailles, I will do all I can to have you released from here.'

Without deigning to understand that after fifteen years here was the first serious chance of freedom before him, Danry, in a delirious speech, began explaining to the lieutenant-general of police that this would be too easy. Why? Leave like that? Without the slightest compensation? Wouldn't the Marquise de Pompadour's heirs, for fear of a lawsuit, highly justified, not have conspired to have him disappear as a troublesome witness, a living proof of their relative's cruelty? He would not leave until he had the compensation due him. How much? 100,000 *livres* at the very least.

Sartine shrugged his shoulders and left the cell without saying a word. Danry was truly fit to be tied. There was nothing left to be done for him, but to consider putting him in Charenton or the Petites-Maisons. It was no longer a question in any case of going to plead his cause at

Versailles. If released, such a rowdy character would surely be capable of the worst extremes and the minister would not fail to hold him, Sartine, responsible. But what was to be done with this prisoner who had become intolerable for the entire staff at the Bastille?

Summer went by without Danry adopting a more sensible attitude. On the contrary, he wrote extremely insulting letters to the lieutenant-general of police and attacked all those who approached him vociferously. You are afraid of the truth, he cried. But woe to all who conspired to keep him shut up there, contrary to justice. Soon the day of reckoning would come. Moreover, Parliament had to be apprised of his case since it was among the many recipients of the petitions sent on their way by his two accomplices.

What Danry did not know was that most of the petitions had never arrived at their destination, because the humble condition of the young Lebrun girls had caused door-keepers and stewards to throw them away as soon as the door was closed upon the visitors. As for the rare ones that were read, their confused, emphatic style immediatley gave the impression that they were the works of a mad man, and the matter ended there.

One evening at the end of August, Danry detained Darragon, who had just brought his supper. Instead of insulting him as usual, he assumed a mysterious air and whispered in his ear: 'Wait, I have something important to say to you.' With a distraught look on his face, and containing his agitation with difficulty, he added: 'I tremble for you.' When Darragon asked him haughtily if he was delirious, Danry replied: 'No, I'm not raving. I've had my papers sent to Parliament for the prosecution of M. de Sartine, and I've received a reply. This is the reason that I tremble for you, because you'll be accused of having followed him. You won't be spared, despite your innocence.'

Two days later, Sartine, to whom Darragon had scrupu-

lously repeated Danry's imprudent words, felt that this
fellow was certainly abusing his good graces and had the
prisoner thrown into the dungeon. Danry went down
singing. 'We'll see,' he shouted, 'if, in a few days, Sartine
has the power to keep me here. He let himself be corrupted
like a scoundrel by money from the Marquis de Marigny
[Mme de Pompadour's brother], but soon he'll be the one
to come down here.'

This was the last straw. Sartine wrote a memorandum
to the new secretary of the King's Household in which pity
at last gave way to anger:

> The longer Danry remains a prisoner, the more wicked
> and wild he becomes. He has made it known that he
> is capable of resorting to the utmost devilry and of
> committing a crime if released. Since 1 July and
> 13 August when I told him still to be patient and that
> the date of his release, which was close at hand, had
> not been decided, there has been no kind of excess,
> foul language, insult or threat that he has not used to
> make himself generally feared. The memory of Mme
> la Marquise is for him a horror and a scourge. He
> lavishes the most villainous epithets upon her, because
> he himself has become a villain in his prison. Even the
> King is not spared his outbursts and insolent remarks.
> After a letter dated 27 July in which he made the most
> atrocious insults and the worst threats against me, after
> that letter, I adopted a humane attitude towards him.
> I scorned his outbursts. He replied with insolent letters
> of such a kind that I had him thrown into a dungeon,
> which he simply made fun of. This man, who is of an
> incredibly enterprising nature, is a major nuisance to
> the Bastille staff. It would be preferable if he were
> transferred to the Castle-keep of Vincennes where there

are fewer prisoners than in the Bastille, and left in oblivion.

'Left in oblivion' . . . What a terrible formula! The *lettre de cachet*, whose effects can be indefinitely prolonged, makes this possible, and this is what, since that time, has made it seem iniquitous in comparison with ordinary justice, even if such cases are rare. Already d'Argenson, who was lieutenant-general of the Paris police at the end of Louis XIV's reign, had used that expression in regard to a debauchee dealing in young boys whose charms he had first tested. The whole of this little circle had been arrested, but d'Argenson, fearing that a public trial, instead of inspiring horror, would encourage certain inclinations, had written to the minister: 'You know that there was no less inconvenience in submitting the accused parties to the rules of ordinary procedure than in concealing their irregular behaviour. Hence I believe that the man called Néel deserves to be transferred to the Bastille to be left in oblivion.'

D'Argenson sometimes substituted a prettier formula for this conclusion, which fell like the executioner's axe. So in the case of a high-ranking couple of advanced age whose domestic fights scandalized Paris, the lieutenant-general of police had concluded in his report to the minister: 'The public is delighted with the scene before it and no one has yet had the kindness to lower the curtain to hide such a ridiculous sight.' Obviously, the *lettre de cachet* itself was able to lower the curtain.

On the night of 15/16 September 1764, after M. de Saint-Florentin had sent a new *lettre de cachet* to the Bastille asking the governor to transfer Danry to the Château de Vincennes, a prisoner steaming with anger and indignation was removed from his cell. The guards, overjoyed to be finally rid of such an unbearable subject, attached a long iron chain to his neck which they slipped between his legs and brutally pulled taut the length of his back before attaching the other end again to his neck. Broken in two, Danry no longer dreamt of complaining, but of alleviating the pain that pierced his body. It was in this state that he arrived a few hours later with a solid escort at the Castle-keep of Vincennes where he was immediately placed in solitary confinement, so great was his reputation as a troublemaker.

8

The Third Escape

But at Vincennes Danry said not another word, even confessing his sins to M. de Guyonnet, the King's lieutenant, and to Laboissière, major of the castle-keep. After a few weeks, the governor reported this marvel to Sartine, who had Danry placed in a normal room. He wanted to encourage him to continue this good conduct. On M. de Guyonnet's advice, Danry wrote Sartine a long letter of apology. The strongly worded letters that had offended him had only been dictated, he explained, as a token of friendship, in order to protect him from ever-present misfortune. He begged pardon in any case if the lieutenant-general of police had been offended by anything he had written.

This submissive attitude deserved a reward. So Danry was restored to a comfortable regime of a fire, candles and even writing material. He was also granted the favour of a daily walk, which at Vincennes was in the moat and lasted for two hours. His gaoler was a veteran, recently demobilized. Danry, who had also been in the army, liked to chat with his guard. One day, during one of their talks, he discovered that the lieutenant-colonel who had been in command of the dragoon regiment at Sedan where his gaoler had served was called M. de Latude. 'What was his name?' Danry asked, his heart pounding. 'Well,' the veteran replied, 'because M. de Latude died in Sedan at the end of January 1761, I remember his name well, for we were on duty and went by carriage to fetch his widow. She had travelled a long way, from Languedoc, I believe.'

From that day on, Danry decided that he was the recognized son of this father who had always ignored him. Since the name was vacant, or so he thought, he was going to rename himself de Latude and be ennobled at the same time. Fate owed him that at least. Unaware that the real name was Vissec de Latude, but remembering that it was a compound name, Danry added the name of a part of Montagnac which he thought belonged to the Latude family: Masers. Thus was Masers de Latude born.

From then on, Danry was to sign all his letters in this way. When he had an idea in his head, he would not let go of it, remorselessly repeating the name until he got his way. He was no longer acquainted with Danry. There had never been a Danry. It was a borrowed name given to him at the Bastille, he would say, to hide his real identity and thus to make his imprisonment appear secret. But now he wanted to be called by his real name: Vicomte Masers de Latude.

Of course, the Vicomte de Latude could no longer accept his freedom on the same conditions as Danry. The sum of 150,000 *livres* and the cross of Saint-Louis were henceforth the condition for his release. Sartine, who received this letter written in a new, and actually noble, tone, was amused. It did not matter if the prisoner was delirious, as long as he remained calm. He wanted to be called Masers de Latude? Let it be Latude.

Danry was disgusted. Latude moved in higher circles. In new letters to Sartine he now evoked, in a learned and protective tone, his ruined fortune, his brilliant, but damaged, career, his family which had been plunged into despair. He went so far as to give the lieutenant-general of police advice as to the advancement of his career. Even better, he wrote a speech for him to deliver at the first audience with the King. 'Take advantage of this moment of respite. Before you get on your horse, the day when peace is celebrated, you should be a Councillor of State.'

Meanwhile, freedom did not come. A year had gone by since the transfer to Vincennes, and Danry's thoughts once again turned to escape. But his reputation was such that he was kept under close watch. Each week, his room was methodically searched and a second younger guard was added to the first to accompany Danry on his daily walk, with orders never to leave him for a single step.

But on 23 November 1765, at four o'clock in the afternoon, a thick fog fell over Vincennes as the daily walk in the moat was nearing its end. Danry realized immediately that it was an excellent opportunity for escaping. He froze in his tracks and turned to his disconcerted guards. Of course he must say something before they grabbed hold of him. 'How do you like this weather, sergeant?' he asked. 'It's very bad, sir,' the sergeant replied civilly.

Then Danry, who had already moved away from his escort, added under his breath: 'I myself find it very good for escaping.' With these words he ran as fast as he could and disappeared from his guards' sight before they had the time to realize what was happening. Danry, literally flying along the moat, had already passed two guards who had only caught sight of him at the last moment, to see him disappearing into the fog. Behind him, everyone shouted: 'Stop! Stop!'

In the moat confusion reigned. The guards ran in all directions, while windows opened and shouts of enquiry came to mingle with the rest of the noise created by the pursuers. Two guards ran smack into each other while a third, thinking he was doing the right thing, fired shots in the air, bringing the excitement to fever pitch. Danry, finally out of the moat, was shooting across the royal courtyard like an arrow when he encountered a group of soldiers turning around in circles. 'Stop! Stop!' cried Danry inspired, pointing frantically into the distance. 'Stop! Stop!' chorused the soldiers, deluded by this old trick, hurling themselves after him. But they were soon outdistanced by this unusually zealous pursuer.

Danry came in sight of the front gate. It was impossible to trick the guard at the entrance. He would automatically take the first person to appear before him for the escapee. And in fact, at the sound of the first shouts, the sentry had placed himself across the passage with rifle and bayonette pointing towards the courtyard. The fugitive appeared. It was Chenu on duty, and moreover, he knew the prisoner. 'Stop, he shouted, 'or I'll stick my bayonette through your body.'

Danry slowed down and quietly approached the guard, saying to him in a calm voice: 'Chenu, your orders are to stop me, not to kill me.' The fugitive approached even closer, ready to surrender. But suddenly he lunged forward like a fiend, knocking poor Chenu over and throwing his rifle away. The first pursuers only had time to see him run off again and disappear into the fog.

Easily hiding in the forest surrounding the castle, Danry waited for nightfall before entering Paris. His first visit was to the two girls with whom he had become acquainted from the top of the Bastille towers. Their greeting was the warmer since they had not seen the prisoner for a long time and had thought that he was dead. Pressed with all sorts of questions, Danry looked through the window at the bleak Bastille where he had spent the best years of his youth. His mind was revolted at such a thought. But now that he was free, he was going to repay those responsible for his imprisonment, and very dearly.

His young friends, the Lebrun young ladies, willingly gave him refuge. But Danry was without the slightest resource, as on his previous escapes. He had fled with his slippers on, without a penny in his pocket.

When he saw the number of his memoranda and letters that were still there or that had been returned because their addressees had not wanted them, Latude realized that the girls had not been equal to their mission, although their zeal was not to be questioned. It was time to take matters into his own hands.

Among many addressees, the Marshal de Noailles looked particularly hopeful. Wasn't it he who had obtained a letter of recommendation for his surgeon upon his demobilization? He had not prepared one letter for him, but a whole basketful. He asked the Marshal de Noailles to continue the honour of his protection and informed him of four major discoveries he had just made: the first, on the real cause of the ocean's ebb; the second, on what causes mountains, without which the terrestrial globe would come to a standstill and within a short period of time turn into glass; the third, on why this same terrestrial globe is continually revolving; the fourth, on what causes water in all the seas to be salty.

Unfortunately, when the two Lebrun girls went to the Rue Saint-Honoré to Marshall de Noailles's home, his secretary absolutely refused to accept so strange a basket. Not to be discouraged, Danry wrote to the Duc de Choiseul, the Minister of War, asking for the advance of 10,000 crowns of the amount owed him for his military project. He also wrote to the lieutenant-general of police to make peace proposals. In return for the 10,000 crowns advanced on the 150,000 *livres* owed him by the royal treasury, he would forget the cruelties of which he had been a victim and 'we'll say no more about it.'

Apart from the outlandishness of such a proposal, Danry underestimated the scandal that his new escape had caused at Versailles. 'I'm furious about Danry's escape,' the minister wrote to the governor of Vincennes the day after the escape, 'and I don't know how I'm going to inform the King about it. Despite all that you have told me, I cannot imagine how in the first place you allowed the prisoner the walk without my authorization. You know how important it was that he should not escape, and so this should never have happened. You do not take a prisoner out of prison in foggy weather, and when he forced the sentry, the latter should have shot him; I must confess I'm extremely pained by this event, and I don't know how the King is going to react.'

The guards on duty that day were all thrown into prison for a long time. M. de Guyonnet, the governor of Vincennes, did not know where to turn to hide his shame. As for Sartine, one familiar with human weaknesses, he did not give up the possibility that Danry would make another mistake. Of course the message that he had received had no address on it this time, but its suggestion was so ridiculous that it was reasonably certain that the escapee would make one of those blunders peculiar to him alone.

And in fact since Sartine had not responded to the signals he had been requested to make at a certain place, the incorrigible Danry arrived on a cold morning on 17 December, at Fontainebleau, having travelled the whole night in one of those ordinary cabs of the Court called 'chamberpots', on account of their resemblance to this receptacle. He immediately went to request an audience with the Duc de Choiseul who would be obliged to see him this time. After a long spell in the waiting room, the Duke's Swiss guard informed him that he would be received. 'At last!', Danry thought as he mentally repeated the magnificent speech he was about to deliver to the minister. A door opened. Danry walked through. He was immediately seized by two police officers.

In the chaise that took the escapee back to Vincennes, the two police officers were astonished. How had he got all the way to Fontainebleau? All the roads leading to it, the avenues to the castle, the entrances to the city, the stage coaches and horse-drawn barges had been under such tight surveillance that one had to be invisible to reach the Duc de Choiseul. Besides, didn't he know that there was no greater crime than daring to go around complaining from one minister to another? And how the devil, the police officers, in brilliant form because of such a great catch, teasingly asked, had the prisoner managed to escape from Vincennes? A weary Danry superbly replied: 'An ox would have done the same as I did.'

9

The Castle-keep of
Vincennes

Danry would certainly have been better off once again
keeping a low profile. Was it really worth pulling off three
ingenious escapes in a row, each time to walk straight back
into the lion's den? The prisoner could not help thinking
sadly of this, locked up again at Vincennes.

Curiously enough, his stay in solitary confinement did
not last long after this last escape. After a few months he
was given a proper room and put on the normal diet. His
daily walk was, however, suppressed once and for all.
Likewise, Sartine did not attempt to find out who had
harboured the runaway, despite a furious desire to punish
all those who had dared lend assistance to this public enemy.
The reasons for this lenient attitude were simple. It was
increasingly believed that the prisoner was subject to visions,
that he was to be pitied more than blamed. Punishment
would only over-excite his deranged state.

As the months, and then the years, went by, Danry did
in fact begin to go mad. His outbursts of anger returned,
more violent than ever. Sartine alone, with the governor
of Vincennes, to whom he retained the right to send letters,
served as an outlet for him: 'The very devil, this is going
a bit too far! I must say, sir, that even if I were to boast
just a little to you, the worst devils in all hell find it difficult
to give you new lessons in cruelty.'

Sometimes the tone was stronger: 'You couldn't find a single person surprised to see you flayed alive, your skin tanned and your body thrown into the sewers. But sir, you mock everything, you don't fear God, the King, or the devil. Sir, you swallow crimes like your mother's milk!'

The governor, who avoided this intolerable prisoner like the plague and who found that Versailles was too interested in the man for his taste, was not treated much better. One day, when he had the bad idea of poking his head through the cell door, he was met by a violent greeting: 'By all the devils in hell, Sir, your visits are rarer than eclipses of the sun. It would be easier to receive a visit from the great Moghol here. Although I frequently make requests to see you, I've seen twelve whole months go by and the only person I've seen is the surgeon who comes to shave me once a week.' The governor withdrew and did not return for a long time.

In prison Danry also wrote his Memoirs. The orderliness of the story was only equalled by the accent of sincerity. Curiously, he was allowed to do this, as the right to pen and paper was mandatory. Better still, it was known that his trunk hid papers that could be dangerous if they came to be circulated in Paris where philosophers held secret cabals. On one occasion, there had been threats to look inside, after the seals placed by the prisoner had been broken. 'Sir,' Danry replied, 'there are certain legal formalities to which you must conform, and you are not permitted to perpetrate violations of this sort.'

It was quite good at Vincennes and the trunk was allowed to fill up with words of revenge without anyone bothering to look. Another time, the prisoner's flute, which was played night and day and got on the nerves of the guards and other prisoners, was confiscated. For years, Danry pleaded, this little instrument had not left him for one moment, dissipating his boredom. Touched by the argument, the new governor of Vincennes, M. de Rougemont, had the flute returned to its owner. But he was asked to play only during the day and not at night at all. 'But, sir,' Danry replied insolently, 'don't you consider that forbidding me my flute is enough to make me want to do just that.'

Indeed, Danry did not give up and was once again contemplating his escape. But reduced to his own means, he could take no more risks, he had been finally deprived of his walks. That was why he had to establish a correspondence with the other prisoners. A difficult task . . . But so long as it was not impossible, Danry would dare to undertake it. He first had to make a hole 5 to 6 metres below in the enormous wall of the keep next to the garden where the prisoners took their walk. Impossible to get into contact with them otherwise, Danry remembered that he had hidden an iron rod in this garden before his impromptu escape. But the walk had been stopped once and for all. If I break a window pane, he thought, it's probable that they'll avoid letting me have a single minute's contact with the workers from outside. Perhaps they'll take me to the garden.

The guess was right. Danry broke two glass panes in his window, making believe that it was an accident. The day after, a glazier was called in, and the prisoner was led down to the garden during repairs. Swift as lightning, Danry recovered the iron rod, still hidden underneath a pile of old abandoned beams, and hid it under his shirt. As he walked back up the stairs with an appearance of calm, Danry was inwardly exultant. At last a plan, a reason to live in this hell that had become his life.

The wall round the castle-keep of Vincennes was as thick as that of the Bastille, and the improvised instrument was too supple to be sufficiently effective. To get through would require twenty-six months of hard work, during which Danry was to give up a hundred times and then begin again. But his determination was rewarded. The hole, made inside the chimney, and hidden in the shadow of the mantle, was covered by some home-made putty which the industrious prisoner could remove and put back at will. A string was made again, out of thread from a sheet and a shirt. At the end, a small piece of wood and a ribbon to attract the attention of the first prisoner to turn up.

The first to swallow the bait was a captain sent to Vincennes for indiscipline and extortion. He saw the ribbon, then the string, took hold of it, and drawing closer to the wall, heard a voice coming from the sky. No, it was not the devil speaking these words, but poor Latude whose sad story he had to hear . . .

Apart from a few exceptional cases of subjects thought to be dangerous, they sent the prisoners to the garden for their walk in turn, merely calling them when it was time to return to their cells. Again, the fact that the guard was manned by invalid soldiers resulted in unquestionably slack surveillance.

In this manner, after a few weeks Danry became acquainted with almost all the resident prisoners, of whom there were not very many. One was there because he had published works that had been banned: another for selling forged lottery tickets without realizing it, he said. An ecclesiastic claimed that he was wrongly accused of seducing the daughter of a notary and getting her pregnant. A man with a feverish voice, who would not tell his name, said that he had come to know of a secret treasure and that the police had tortured him to find out where it was hidden; but he would not tell them. Another was a magistrate from the Parliament of Rennes who had been arrested by *lettre de cachet* after the parliamentary revolt against the royal authority.

Danry had found his man. He tried to interest him in his cause, pointing out to him that his case was the best example of abuse of authority. The magistrate agreed. 'Will you talk about it once you are released from here?' – 'Of course, but the Parliament of Rennes is not the Parliament of Paris. You would have to put your case to a councillor in the Paris district.' Danry foamed with anger and almost insulted the invisible speaker. As if he could choose his magistrates! Was this really the representative of justice who, suffering like him from tyranny and iniquity, was speaking to him of jurisdictions and authority? As soon as he was released from this damned place, he would more likely go to tell the president of Parliament the story of an innocent man imprisoned without trial for twenty-eight years! The Breton magistrate promised he would help, but knew already that he would do nothing. If he hated the fact that the government snapped its fingers at justice, he hated it even more when someone talked to him in such tones.

Correspondence was also exchanged with a few prisoners through the hole in the wall. But whether talk was on political matters or escape plans, Danry only encountered in those speaking to him a feeble echo of his own aspirations. All hoped for freedom sooner or later and many could even reasonably calculate a date of release. Sometimes it was the lieutenant-general of police himself who had indicated it. Why then take up the cause of this prisoner who had nothing more to lose, and why embark on a desperate act with him? Despite his fixed idea, Danry finally realized this. No one would help him to escape. And he soon returned to his solitude.

The years again went by. It was really meant to be forgotten that Danry was in Vincennes. Since his recapture, he had not left his room and time no longer had any meaning to him. Only Christmas reminded him that another year had gone by. How many Christmases since his last escape? He did not know. Ten perhaps . . . How old was he now? Forty or fifty? But what did it matter! In the gloomy apathy that had taken hold of him, reason was no longer more than a flicker of light, increasingly weaker and weaker.

The year 1774 could have been a year of liberation. In fact, this was the year in which, on 10 May, Louis XV suddenly died in the midst of general hostility. It was also the year in which, in August, Jean-Charles-Pierre Le Noir succeeded Gabriel de Sartine as head of the Paris police force.

In opposition to d'Argenson's severity or Sartine's cynicism, Le Noir was a liberal, a gentle man who would even be reproached for his lack of firmness. Formerly chief of petitions, then intendant of the Généralité of Limoges, where he had demonstrated his talent for organisation, he had assumed his new functions with the best of intentions. In his *Tableau of Paris*, Mercier, usually so fierce, would say of him: 'He has often changed from a minister of compassion and indulgence into a minister of justice and rigour, and public order has not suffered from this.'

All the conditions were therefore present to obtain a favour that twenty-five years in prison amply justified. But it was when he should have written that Danry no longer wrote . . . For several years he had said nothing, made no more demands, spending his days reading or stretched on his bed staring at the ceiling.

After contemplating for months on end the high ceiling with its blackened beams and enormous spiders' webs, you finished up seeing strange things there. Among the different books given to him to keep his mind occupied, he came across a few dealing with witchcraft. Danry read them over and over again. Now, he had finally realized what was really strikingly obvious. Only the demons conjured up by the witch Pompadour and then by her brother magician, the Marquis de Marigny, could have been capable of prolonging his detention indefinitely through their perpetual intervention.

On one occasion, he emerged from his despair to try to convince the King's lieutenant at Vincennes who had agreed to come and listen to him. But the conversation got off to a bad start: 'Sir, will you have enough time to write down all I have to say to you?' – 'Sir,' replied the weary officer, 'I will gladly grant you an hour.' 'What! An hour?' the prisoner replied in a complete rage. 'You must stay with me for two or three weeks. And this is only because I noticed when you interrogated me after my escape that you wrote very fast. So this will not be too much time . . .' Furious, the King's lieutenant walked out on Danry and went to complain to the governor in a manner typical of his Norman origin: 'Not everyone would be pleased by this proposal, and I am among the number.' It was finally one of the lieutenant-general of police's officers who had to perform the unpleasant task. Danry asked him also to stay three weeks, but the officer only granted him the morning for the time being. At this, Danry began to explain to him that with 180 magic spells to explain to him and have copied down, there would hardly be enough time that day.

He then took out of a bag a pile of papers covered with indecipherable characters. 'Those under the spell', he declared, 'are first you, who have received 50,000 crowns from the late Marquise de Pompadour to have me held here in the keep. M. de Marigny, her brother in witchcraft, continues to pay the pension for the same reason. A spell has also been cast on M. de la Vrillière, the new minister, and on the new lieutenant-general of police, who is more particularly under the influence of that great expert in satanic sciences, the sorcerer Sartine. The death of His Majesty is also even more obviously due to sorcery, because it was through the King's having made a promise in writing to

Mme de Coislin to dismiss the Marquise and take her afterwards for his mistress that a demon caused the King's assassination, the Marquise having found out about the plan against her interests.'

At the end of an hour of this sort of talk, the officer tried to break off: 'Sir, I do not believe in sorceries at all. They are popular misconceptions which nowadays no one believes in any longer.' But for Danry, this was a little short. 'Sir,' he replied taking hold of his arm, 'I can't show you the demon in person, but I'm really sure I can convince you, with what this memorandum contains, that the late Marquise de Pompadour was a witch and that the Marquis de Marigny, her brother, is still in contact today with the demons.'

Without skipping a line, Danry read to him the very long memorandum. He then wanted to read another. The officer thought that he would go mad himself if he did not try something. But the prisoner must not be annoyed either – he was pacing up and down the room with great strides and occasionally raising his arm into the air from time to time, continuing to read, with fiery cheeks.

Suddenly, the officer was struck with a brilliant idea. Assuming an air of the greatest interest, he abruptly interrupted the reading of the latest memorandum which was going to be even longer than the previous one. 'What was the name you said there earlier?' Danry could no longer recall, getting mixed up himself in his morass of papers. 'The Chevalier de La Roche-Gérault?' he ventured. 'Yes, that's it. I must go and tell M. Le Noir of this immediatley.' And the officer rushed straight to the door. Before disappearing for ever, he fiercely ordered Danry, who was trying to tell him something: 'Write a paper about this knight.'

The officer faithfully reported to Le Noir and confessed his trick, adding: 'Danry is waiting impatiently for you to order me to go and stay with him these three weeks, and I would be very upset if you should feel like doing so.' There was no longer any doubt. The prisoner had gone mad. They would have to consider his transfer from Vincennes to Petites-Maisons, or rather to Charenton, which harboured the insane, but also criminals, and where monks took good care of their residents.

In fact, Danry remained dangerous. Had not a kind of lantern of oiled paper and a lighter been found recently in his room after it had been darkened to cure him of his rage for writing? With this lighting, he had managed, despite all odds, to write new memoranda on bits and pieces of cloth with his own blood. Had he not also kept the Vincennes physician, M. de Lassaigne, prisoner in his room one day, after requesting that he come for his hernia? Trapped between the door and the trunk by Danry who begged him to intervene for him in the name of science, the poor man had to be extracted with tremendous force. Afterwards, he swore that he would never return to see such a maniac, 'except to establish his death'.

The year 1775 arrived without Danry's state improving in the slightest. It was nevertheless in this first year of Louis XVI's reign that Malesherbes, former president of the Court of Aid and director of the Library, disgraced at the end of Louis XIV's reign because of his liberal ideas, had just been recalled as secretary to the King's Household. So here was this protector of philosophers, this outspoken enemy of *lettres de cachet*, who had become the minister to whom the Paris lieutenant-general of police had to report.

Malesherbes was hardly in office as head of a ministry whose brief life he could foresee than he decided to embark on a tour of inspection of prisoners locked up by *lettres de cachet*. With his twenty-six years of imprisonment, Danry's case did not fail to draw his attention. So one of the first visits in his inspection of the state prisons was to this prisoner who could surely claim a quick release after such a record of detention. But the dossier mentioned attacks of madness over the past few years.

As soon as he had visited the Bastille, as was customary, and not without giving instructions for the immediate release of several prisoners, the minister went to the Castle-keep of Vincennes. There, inspection by the supervisory minister was so rare that a real preparation for action was under way. Having only been notified the day before, an extremely worried governor desperately tried to contact the lieutenant-general of police for advice. But in vain. And now on this fine morning at the end of August, all these gentlemen were there, putting on a forced smile. The governor tried to smile too, but he knew all too well that his career was at stake.

As was to be expected of this opponent of the forces of law and order, the first person the minister wanted to see was Danry. He asked to be taken to his cell and insisted, despite warnings of caution, on being left alone with the prisoner. The sight of this prematurely aged man who had difficulty in getting up deeply moved him. Here was a sad example of those endless detentions against which he had fought when he was president of the Court of Aid. The prisoner should speak up without fear. He was in the presence of his minister who wanted only his good. Otherwise, why would he be there?

Danry first complained that up until then they had refused to listen to him. He was not even allowed anything to write with. For years, he had not left his cell for one moment. It might be deduced that he was guilty of some great crime. But he was not. He had only committed the error some twenty-six years back of wanting to be kind to the Marquise de Pompadour. Now, if everyone knew that she was the King's mistress and that she lost no time before ruling over France, few people were aware that she was also a witch. Wasn't this the least that was needed to kill the late King in effigy?

Soon, Danry continued, the minister, the lieutenant-general of police and the entire staff at the Bastille in turn all had a spell cast on them. Of course, Mme de Pompadour was dead but the Minister was well aware that these kinds of powers were handed down in families. And today, he knew very well that it was M. de Marigny, the Pompadour's brother, who was keeping up the sorcery. The last spell to date was that put upon the president of the Parliament of Paris who was going to raise his case and thus cause the scandal of his imprisonment to break. The Minister must also certainly be aware that the sorcerer de Marigny was responsible for the disappearance of the Marshal de Noailles, who was his protector.

Malesherbes listened and observed this reddened face, this fixed look, these jerky gestures. The reports had been only too right. The man was mad without any doubt. Using the excuse that he still had to visit the other prisoners, the minister interrupted Danry's endless speech, but promised that he would work actively towards his release from there. Danry wanted to kiss his feet, but Malesherbes was already knocking at the door which was opened immediately to worried faces. The minister was caught up by helpful hands and the heavy door was quickly shut on the prisoner who, raising his voice of thunder, continued to pursue his worthy audience with his talk.

After his inspection of the Bastille and Vincennes, Malesherbes wrote in his report to the King: 'Danry, Thorin and Maréchal are all three totally insane as stated in notes given to me, and the first two showed unquestionable signs in my presence.' On 23 September 1775 a *lettre de cachet* signed by the King and Lamoignon de Malesherbes ordered

Danry's transfer to Charenton 'on the grounds of derange-
ment of the mind'. 'The King will pay his pension', the
order added laconically.

Early in the morning of 27 September M. de Rougemont,
the governor of Vincennes, entered Danry's cell with two
officers. 'The minister', an officer told him, 'thinks you
should gradually get used to breathing a freer air. He is
sending you to a monastery for a few months, which is
not very far from here. I have received orders to take you
there.'

Danry could not believe his ears. Was this the release
that he had awaited daily since the minister's visit? 'Officer,
I beg you, please don't be angry with what I'm about to
say.' – 'Speak up, say whatever you please. I'll not be
angry.' – 'Well, I see very clearly that the demon has already
taken possession of you.'

10

At Charenton with the Insane

Tightly handcuffed, Danry was put into a carriage with another prisoner, who was paler and more emaciated than a ghost. Also in chains, the man politely enquired where they were going and then proceeded to explain that he was from the Swiss canton of Friburg and that his name was Thorin. Already Danry liked him and was beginning the recital of his misfortunes when his neighbour interrupted him, visibly elsewhere, to ask him in his calm voice for news 'of the hemisphere in which they were at the moment'. These strange words, along with Thorin's fixed look, caused Danry to shudder. The man looked mad. He hoped that he was not going to a place for maniacs instead of being taken to a convalescent home?

After quite a short journey, the two prisoners arrived at a huge building surrounded by an abundance of leafage. From its elevated position could be viewed lower down a magnificent panorama of fields and meadows through which ran a large river which Danry supposed was the Seine. Monks greeted him with gentleness and kindness, immediately removing his fetters and asking him to follow them to his room where he would be able to rest. Already Danry felt reassured. His encounter with this man, Thorin, who was also untied, and certain ambiguous statements by the officers had given him a disturbing impression which was now going away.

Danry was about to inform the monks walking in front of him in a large courtyard surrounded by buildings, of the terrible suspicion that had scratched the surface of his mind, when he caught sight of some men whose behaviour once again intrigued him. One was dancing in a most extravagant manner, another, wearing a crown of leaves, was walking with an air of grotesque majesty. A third was standing underneath a covered courtyard as though petrified in a position of prayer. Danry grabbed one of the monks' sleeves and asked in astonishment who these men were. The friar leading him then replied that they were madmen. 'Madmen?' Danry shouted angrily. 'What! I'm in a . . .' – 'But, sir,' the monk continued in a soft tone, jingling his keys the while in a most sinister way, 'you must know that you're here in Charenton.'

Initially a small hospital at the time of its foundation in 1641, Charenton was run by monks belonging to the order of the Charity friars. This order, created by Saint Jean de Dieu, then came to be established in France to devote itself especially to the care of the insane. In the reign of Louis XVI, the Charity friars owned thirty-eight mental institutions in France and the colonies, of which that of Charenton was the most famous. A hundred and twenty criminals were locked up in this model establishment with separate units for disturbed lunatics, for harmless lunatics and finally for criminals placed there by *lettres de cachet* for various motives ranging from debauchery to petty crime.

Charenton, whose name by the reign of Louis XV had become synonymous with a lunatic asylum, nevertheless deserved better than its reputation. The institution, with fees of 600–1,000 *livres* a year, only accepted individuals from the upper bourgeoisie, even from the nobility. Rules and regulations were less severe than in most other detention centres, and much time was allowed for leisure and walks in the huge terraced gardens overlooking the Marne. Two separate regimes did, however, coexist: detention and semi-liberty. They were both accompanied by the capacity religious homes have for shifting from kindness to repression in very subtle steps.

Another feature, discretion was the form. New arrivals were often brought in at night, and everyone upon arrival was given a pseudonym in order to preserve family honour. No Masers de Latude or Danry here, but a name that said a good deal about the recommendations of the governor of Vincennes: Danger.

After Danry had been carried, in a semi-conscious state, to a tiny room entirely furnished with a small corner bed attached to the wall, he was left alone for a minute. Then the same friar, accompanied by two gaolers, entered his cell and handed him a shirt and a cap, ordering him to take off all his clothes, put on the new garments and then go to bed. Danry, recovering his senses, pointed out that it was only two o'clock and tried to resist. But seeing that they were prepared to use violence, he gave in without saying a word. His new guards then left, carefully locking the door behind them and taking away his clothes for inspection.

In the depths of despair, Danry realized that he had done no more than change his torture and tormenters. But why put him in a madhouse? He was not mad. Did his persecutors want to debase him that much more and degrade him in his own eyes by taking away the only thing left to him: his capacity as a man? Not far from there, a terrible cry caused him to sit up in his bed. He went to the window, which was shut with a heavy grating. But all he saw was a tiny ray of light. Now there was no longer a single cry, but a clamour, which struck him with horror. Dozens of madmen were screaming a few feet away, making the walls tremble with heavy blows.

A few hours later, the sound of the door opening interrupted the course of his dark thoughts. The same friar was returning his clothes. He threw them on the bed and told Danry that he could get up and get dressed. Then, still without a word of explanation, he was led down the corridor where the well-behaved lunatics were, to a room with a slightly greater degree of comfort. The bed was small, but a table and chair, a pedestal table holding a washing bowl and pitcher, not forgetting the inevitable chamberpot, completed the furnishing. The window had bars on the outside only, and opened onto a courtyard dotted with linden trees. Indeed, everything breathed order and cleanliness.

It was six o'clock in the evening when the shutter let into the door was opened. It was time for supper, which consisted of a piece of roast mutton, a little white bread, wine and water. The mutton was scarcely cooked, the bread stale and the wine disgusting. Danry was already beginning to regret the food at the Bastille and Vincennes which he had criticized so loudly. There the wine had been quite good and he was given a bottle at every meal. Over the years, Danry had become accustomed to it, and also to walking with long strides in the vast rooms of the Bastille and Vincennes. Impossible to take two steps here without bumping into something. Besides, the other prisoners could be heard moving around in the near-by cells. That was also something that bothered Danry, who had become used to the deathly silence of his former prisons.

Nevertheless, this relatively indiscriminate mixing facilitated contact with the other prisoners. Indeed, in most religious detention centres, the custom was to open all the door-shutters after the noon and evening meals so that the prisoners could talk to one another. But the fact that the detainees could not see each other, as well as the relative distance of the cells, obliged everyone to talk loudly – almost to shout. How could dishonest talk be imagined in these conditions, when a friar or a gaoler could be in the corridor at any time? Besides, eavesdropping on conversations enabled the monks to monitor the mental state of each prisoner, by keeping a careful record of the whims and deliriums of every one.

As early as the first evening, Danry could hear that questions were being asked about him. Who was the newcomer who was not allowed out for walks? Surely he was some dangerous madman . . . then Danry ran to his door-shutter shouting that he was neither dangerous nor mad, and that nevertheless he had been in irons for the past twenty-seven years for having wanted to save the late Marquise de Pompadour from a plot that he had uncovered. 'The Spanish Inquisition never sentenced a man to such torture,' Danry added. 'Welcome,' one of his neighbours said, 'We thought you were asleep. You have indeed suffered much, and the length of your detention fills us with horror and pity.'

Another prisoner who said he was called Saint-Magloire explained to Danry, who was surprised to see that his companions did not appear very mad at all, that lunatics were not the only ones locked up at Charenton, but that there were also some 'bad boys'. The other's name was Saint-Luc. He apologized for not being able to tell his real name, but he was of noble blood and had promised to preserve the family honour by not mentioning a name that also belonged to others. He had merely committed an 'indiscretion' and had to stay there for only a few months. Besides, he could go wherever he wanted in the courtyards and corridors and soon would visit the man he already knew was called 'Danger'.

In fact, the day after his arrival, because Danry was the

only one locked up in his room, Saint-Luc and several other prisoners who were free to move around in the corridor came to his door to keep him company. They smiled at each other through the narrow door-shutter. Danry asked a thousand questions about everything that had happened in the world. His ignorance of current events amused, and at the same time moved, the little group. Couldn't it be said that this man had returned from the depths of hell?

Saint-Luc also gave him information about Charenton. It was like everyone said – a mental asylum. Some were in a continual state of insanity and madness. They were locked up and sometimes chained in narrow stalls located in an underground corridor which had been nicknamed the catacombs. Yes, they were the ones you could sometimes hear screaming. Yes, of course, these surroundings were horrible, but you got used to it.

As for the insane, who periodically went into fits of rage, they were allowed to roam around the place freely. They were only locked up when they were about to go into this regrettable state. Others were only slightly, and sometimes amusingly, disturbed. Their state was often caused by a single idea or a unique object. In all other aspects, they appeared normal and sound of mind. These were usually allowed to leave their room, mix with the others and gather in groups, to take walks throughout the entire house, and some were even allowed to go out during the day. Their treatment was so gentle that they usually were very cheerful.

Danry, who was always putting his foot in it, asked one of the prisoners humming behind his door in which category he was. But far from being offended by this question, everyone laughed. Saint-Luc kindly explained again to poor Danger that there were also young men of important families at Charenton who were sent there for petty offences. It was the lot of all those talking to him at that moment, and even if there was in their company one of those peaceful, cheerful madmen who were free to move around the place, it would scarcely be charitable to remind him of his state. Danry willingly agreed and promised not to make any more remarks of the kind. Saint-Luc, on his part, promised that he would do all he could (something that was not to be underestimated) at least to obtain permission for Danger to receive visits in his room from some of the residents.

And in fact a few days later, one Sunday after dinner, a gaoler opened his door. A few of the inmates had come with their musical instruments to give him a concert. Saint-Luc was also there and introduced himself with great civility. His embroidered clothes, the whiteness of his stockings, his beautifully curled wig showed that he was from the best part of society.

When the concert began, it gave Danry a surprise. He was already in a very happy state at this charming gathering. None of the musicians knew how to play, and the rough sound made by the violins would have made him run away if he had not been doubly a prisoner. For a baton, the conductor of the orchestra used a broom-handle which he employed to hit the musicians whenever he wanted to beat time. It was only then that Danry understood that he was being given a concert by madmen.

The concert lasted a long time and when it was finally over, the conductor asked if perchance Danger knew how to play an instrument – wind if possible, because in their chamber orchestra, there were only strings. Perhaps the harmony suffers a little because of this', he added.

Danry looked with terror at his flageolet which had been returned by the monks after inspection and which he had placed in full view on the little toilet table. But luckily nobody noticed it. The better to draw his visitors' attention away, Danry exclaimed that he had been thrilled by the concert. 'Wonderful', one of them replied. 'We'll come back and give you one every Sunday'.

As the musicians solemnly filed out of the door, with Saint-Luc in turn making his farewells, Danry was moved to tears. In the end this grotesque cacophony had been for him the sweetest of all music, that of the company of humankind rediscovered at last, albeit with idiots. Besides, wasn't their solicitude a thousand times more worthy of the name of humanity than the cruelty or indifference of all those who had kept him shut up for twenty-seven years? Wasn't the screeching of violins of friendship worth as much as the grating of the enormous bolts of the Bastille and the great tower of Vincennes?

The instructions from the lieutenant-general of police were so severe that the father prior, despite Danry's good behaviour and constant requests of Saint-Luc, could not bring himself to allow the slightest freedom in the place. If neither the Bastille nor Vincennes had prevented this man from escaping, he argued, what would happen at Charenton, which was not even fenced round. In contrast, the prior was quite willing that Danry should be given reading and writing materials and that visits to his room should continue.

Danry immediately took up his pen again and resumed his libellous writing. He had completely forgotten about them since entering Charenton. He took advantage of the occasion to raise himself to a dignified rank and signed all his letters: 'Vicomte Masers de Latude, engineer, geographer, pensioner of the King at Charenton'.

However, an incident was about to serve as a pretext to the obstinate Saint-Luc for Danger to be allowed to leave his isolation. The winter of 1775–6 was so harsh that one morning one of the residents, who had also been shut up in his room, was found frozen to death. The indignant

Saint-Luc immediately went to petition the prior. Did he want to take the risk of Danger dying like that, weakened as he was by so many years of captivity? Then what would the minister say! If they had wanted the prisoner killed off, they would have disposed of the matter long ago. That meant, in some way or other, that Versailles wanted Danger to live. The father prior, greatly disturbed by the relevance of the argument, gave permission for Danry to take his meals in the room of a resident called Saint-Bernard, where there was always a fire and therefore much company.

This man, Saint-Bernard, was the eternal kind of prisoner always engaged in business dealings and involved in all sorts of more or less legal activities. He made straw goods, bred birds, bought and sold wine, clothes, toilet articles. Money also circulated, and also news sheets which were nevertheless forbidden. In Saint-Bernard's room which had become the meeting-place of almost all the residents, it was also possible to place orders for fruit, pastries and even cooked dishes delivered by a caterer.

The two men hit it off immediately, and on the first evening Danry ordered some meat, fruit, sugar and most important of all a wine that was less bitter than the one served by the friars. In exchange, he had sold Saint-Bernard an outfit at a good price and two pairs of stockings from the rich Bastille wardrobe he had put together at the King's expense. Danry would also like a little brandy. But speaking of that, where were all these articles?

'Follow me', said Saint-Bernard, taking a key hanging on the wall. He then led Danry to the cell directly in front of his. He turned the key in the keyhole and stood aside to allow Danry to enter a room with every imaginable article a prisoner could dream of neatly arranged on shelves. There were clothes and linen, tobacco in enormous quantity, toilet articles, oil, tea, sugar, bottles of wine and brandy, not to mention various mysterious boxes and a gigantic trunk which took up most of the back wall. Various straw and wicker objects hung from the ceiling alongside tiny cages of twittering birds.

'But, dear Sir,' exclaimed Danry, 'what have you done to get this room?' Saint-Bernard smiled gently and chose the articles requested. He then carefully locked the door behind him and confided: 'You suspect that the residents are not my best customers. The friars on the other hand greatly appreciate my modest services. As you know, they hardly ever get a chance to go into town for their small purchases.'

And so Danry, who took his meals at Saint-Bernard's and joyfully depleted his wardrobe in exchange for all kinds of dainties, often saw the resident monks who came to talk in the evening and then disappeared for a moment with Saint-Bernard.

As the months went by, Danry's status improved. Soon, he was able to go to a huge heated room where the inmates played billiards, cards and backgammon. Sometimes small bets were placed, and whoever ran out of money went to borrow by pawning something with Saint-Bernard. Sometimes Danry was even allowed by one of the monks, a regular member, to go and take the air for a few minutes when night had fallen, in a narrow courtyard surrounded by high walls. There Danry breathed freely, stared up at the stars and caught himself trying to conjure up a way to escape.

At the beginning of autumn 1776, one year after his arrival at Charenton, Danry , who had conducted himself irreproachably, saw a further improvement in his status. The father prior was interested in this strange person whose twenty-seven years of captivity filled him with compassion. And then he had been entrusted with a prisoner whom he

had been told was a madman. Yet nobody in Charenton
had been able to detect a sign of insanity in this fellow.
Besides, the superior flattered himself, it was possible that
the good treatment dispensed at Charenton had brought
about a happy revolution in the course of the illness. It
would not be the first or last time. So the good father had
sent a report to the minister estimating that Danry's insanity
in Vincennes had only been temporary and that his
improvement perhaps gave grounds for thinking now of
his release.

But Danry always seemed to encounter misfortune, for
M. de Malesherbes had just resigned, having failed to get
his ideas for reform going. The proceedings were therefore
cut short. But at least, the superior of Charenton decided,
Danry had been given the freedom of the place.

What joy Danry felt when one fine morning the doors
of his room were opened for good! At first he was afraid
to go out into the corridor, where his companions were
there waiting for him; they too were just as thrilled. Danry
suddenly started running like a child, hugging everyone,
then plunging out into the open air. There he beheld the
distant countryside and admired with delight the gardens,
vineyards and trees. But already the fresh September air
and the excitement almost caused him to faint. He had
almost to be carried back to his room. The door nevertheless
was to remain wide open, as a promise of bliss.

Danry needed only a few days to familiarize himself with
this new-found freedom. He formed a happy band with his
companions, especially with Saint-Luc. But they made sure
that they did not displease the Charity friars who were
responsible for their keep. They continued to meet in Saint-
Bernard's room and in the room of a young knight, the
son of a lieutenant-colonel. Danry, who was no longer
called Danger, but Masers, had assumed his role of
gentleman so well that the sight of his noble, easy manner,

the effect of his conversation, full of family memories, would dispel any doubt that he had been that brilliant civil engineer in his younger days, victimized by the whim of the King's favourite. Danry believed it himself and was so happy with his life that he did not even think of escaping any more. Besides, wasn't the prior acting to obtain his freedom from the new minister?

The only thing that bothered Danry was the presence of several lunatics in the group. One of them had been a Grenadier captain in the Picardy regiment and now thought he was God. He was intelligent and had turned out to be an excellent comrade in all respects. But he was inflexible on the subject of his divinity. Nevertheless, in their kindness, the fathers allowed him to attend Mass. Wasn't the Kingdom of Heaven wide open to the poor in spirit? During the service, he was a model of piety, as was becoming when one was God. But when it was time for the Elevation, he pointedly turned his back to the altar and to the celebrant priest. One day, Danry reproached him for this. 'I can't help it,' he replied, 'I can't bear seeing myself eaten alive.'

Another, a lawyer from the Auvergne who had lost his reason through love, kept bowing to everyone, asking for pardon. Yet another was a former monk who had been driven mad by an excess of self-denial. He also wanted to grovel all the time, seeing this as his only way towards eternal salvation. No sooner had he met Danry, who had a great reputation at Charenton as a martyr, than he pledged himself to his service, following him round like a faithful dog.

Neither Danry nor the gaolers could prevent him from making his bed, sweeping his room and thinking up all sorts of little services to perform for him. Danry told him one morning that he had not slept well because of a flea. The poor madman bravely locked himself up in the room with the loathsome creature, declaring that he would not come out until he had killed it. And in fact, a few hours later, a shout of triumph was heard, followed by a wild stampede in the corridor. Breathless and triumphant, the hunter brought Danry his catch, crushed tightly in the palm of his hand.

But life among the insane was not always such fun. Sometimes there were fights and brawls. The friars and gaolers would immediately jump on the rebels. They would tie up their hands and haul them off to a large vat of cold water into which their heads were ducked repeatedly. This punishment could also be inflicted on prisoners considered sane. The madmen whose fits of rage risked lasting longer were taken down to an underground room known as the catacombs, and they were chained up and in some cases put into an iron cage. When the crisis ended, they could go back to their residential quarters.

One day, a lunatic returned from the catacombs told Danry about a raving madman who had been down there for years and had never been brought up again. He was in fact in a constant state of disorder, and was chained up inside a cage. No one had ever been able to calm his agitation or restore his peace of mind. He was formerly a prisoner in the Bastille. His name was Dalègue, or Allègre.

When Danry heard this, he had difficulty in controlling the feelings that swept over him. He wanted to see his former companion straight away and ran to the friar in charge of the cells in the catacombs. But the friar refused. No one could visit the raving madman without the father prior's permission. Danry, with tears in his eyes, immediately went to petition him, but the prior had no choice but to tell him the horrible truth. Allègre, for the man down there was indeed he, had been condemned by Versailles to perpetual secrecy. A year or two ago, his mother had written the Bastille wanting to know what had become of her son. The chief of police had sent the letter to the father prior with instructions that should a new letter arrive directly at Charenton, he 'should beware of telling whether the prisoner existed or not.'

But Danry did not give up so easily. For weeks, he laid siege to the father prior's office, arguing that perhaps the sight of his former companion would stun poor Allègre and cause him to regain his reason. Of course, the father reflected, it would not be the first time such a miracle had occurred, and besides, the instructions from Versailles concerned people from the outside, not the residents who were fated to come into contact with one another. Proof of this was that Danger, despite the precautions taken, had ended up finding out about Allègre's presence at Charenton.

In the end, Danry was allowed to see his former companion. The way down to the catacombs was terrifying. His nostrils were immediately assaulted by a terrible stench. In a vast underground room wooden huts stood in a line on each side of a path bordered by two gutters flowing with filth. The sound of chains rattling against the walls of the stalls, muffled grunting, laughing and sudden screaming caused the visitor to recoil in horror, unaccustomed as he was to these places. And to see Allègre, he had to go right to the end, walking over rotten straw and sensing the nervousness of the raving madmen gradually filling the entire underground room.

Allègre was in an iron cage, chained to the openwork wall. Danry had thought that he was going to rediscover a friend after twenty years of forced separation. All he saw was an appalling skeleton with a beard and tousled hair of a tremendous length. Haggard eyes were shrunk into an emaciated face. Rags and tatters hung loosely on his body.

Obeying only the dictates of his heart, Danry insisted that the door be opened. He entered the cage and tried to embrace his companion, who brutally pushed him back. The gaoler had already rushed in to rescue the visitor from there and carefully locked the cage again. With tears of despair in his eyes, Danry, shaking the iron bars of the cage, shouted: 'It's me, Danry. Don't you recognize your old friend? Have you forgotten the night we escaped from the Bastille?' Allègre cast a long terrifying look at Danry, before saying in empty tones: 'I am God.'

11

Forty Days

In the spring of 1777 Danry was set to break the record in France for detention in the King's prisons, with a total of twenty-eight years, and the authorities began to find this somewhat disquieting. The father superior of Charenton, for his part, relentlessly raised the question of the release of Danry, who had shown no sign of madness, or even of insubordination, in the eighteen months he had been there. Besides, the authorities were now willingly agreeing to requests for the release of prisoners detained by *lettres de cachet*. In fact in these early days of his reign Louis XVI expressed the desire to make the regime more flexible, and Malesherbes's departure did not jeopardize that new policy which was in line with the newly growing philanthropic movement.

For Danry the fact that Mme de Pompadour had now been dead for twelve years, leaving behind her half-forgotten memories, was another element that pleaded in favour of his liberation. The only problem was that the monarchy, in its wisdom, only agreed to release individuals who had someone to vouch for them. This was a means of avoiding recidivism, with some effect. How was it possible to guarantee that an adventurer like Danry, who had no 'hearth or home' would not, once freed, again indulge in some unfortunate scheme? Don't the same causes produce the same effects? Danry had already been asked on several occasions the names of his protectors and friends, the circumstances of his means and his hopes. But, Danry had nothing. He was nothing.

This was what Danry thought as he continued to lead what was generally a quite enjoyable life amid the little society at Charenton, of which he was now a fully integrated member. Since the traumatic encounter with his former companion, the man who was no longer called Danger, but Masers, had changed. What good was it, he thought, to try to escape again? Oh it wouldn't be difficult! No ropes to weave, no walls to break through. He was surrounded by countryside, which could be reached as soon as he opened the door of his room. But wasn't there another way, a kind of legal escape? He needed a guarantor? That was no obstacle; he could make one up . . .

But first he admitted that he had to be very careful that no one should think that he was mad. More than one companion in his captivity whom he thought to be of sound mind had suddenly turned out to be mad: Saint-Fabien had confided to him one evening that he was the Holy Spirit. Another day the inseparable Justin and Nantes confessed that one was the Emperor of Germany and the other the Tsar of Russia. As for Rennes, who wanted to be recognized as Emperor of the Turks, he only renounced his empire after a plunge into a freezing cold bath. Even some of the words of the amiable Saint-Luc seemed strange at times. Despite this, the Charity friars had never appeared to pay much attention to these moments of delirium, speaking to every resident as they would to a sane man.

Now, on several occasions already, the prior had insidiously interrogated him on the subject of witchcraft. Only recently, he had again asked him what he thought of a newly arrived resident who was continually asking Father Prudence to bless him and chase away a devil that he had in his body. 'We don't know what to do with this fellow,' the superior added, thinking aloud. 'Perhaps he is crazy but there are real cases of possession, when the devil chooses to live in the body of a Christian no madder than you or me. What do you think of this, Masers?'

Danry had almost said what he had been so carefully hiding since he had arrived at Charenton, since he had heard the screaming of the madmen in the catacombs. That is, that it was clear that sorcery had never been better characterized than that of which he continued to be a victim. The same demon that had begun with the Pompadour witch had continued with the Marigny wizard. The departure of M. de Malesherbes, the frenetic behaviour that possessed Allègre by day and night and especially his own presence here, were they not additional proof? But a twinkle in the prior's eyes restrained Danry. Today, when he thought back on the incident, he congratulated himself on his prudence. He would have barely uttered a word before the prior would say: 'Good heavens, there was good reason for sending Masers here. He is mad, and I was terribly wrong to intercede for his freedom.'

Danry knew very well that he was not mad, since the sorcery of which he was victim had been real from the beginning. But who would believe him? Besides, who was to say that demons had not taken hold of the prior's senses without his knowledge? It had taken years for him, Danry, to realize that he was the magicians' prisoner. Caution therefore, and silence.

No more letters, since by these he had only managed to irritate the minister of the King's Household and the lieutenant-general of police. No, he had to wager everything on his good relations with the friars and the father superior. And then he had to settle this problem of finding someone to vouch for him.

A new arrival, the Chevalier de Moyria, who had entered

Charenton at the beginning of 1777, would provide him with an opportunity. A native of Béziers, a member of a very good family, he was there for having wanted to take up his sword against his brother – a minor offence which would only cost the young nobleman a few months in prison. Danry immediately declared himself his protector, introducing him to the privileged company that revolved around Saint-Bernard and Saint-Luc. He himself, he explained at once to the Chevalier, was not Masers, but Viscount Masers de Latude, engineer. He was, like him, from the region of Languedoc, and had been the victim of a conspiracy that had kept him locked up in the King's prisons for the past twenty-eight years.

At the same time Danry addressed the following letter to a certain Maître Caillet, who was the royal notary in Montagnac:

'My dear friend, I would bet ten to one that you think I'm dead. See how wrong you are: I'm still alive and what's more, it's only up to you that before this carnival is over, we may eat a good hare together. How happy I should be if you could tell me the wonderful news that my dear mother is still alive; but I shouldn't have such grandiose ideas! However, since she knew very well while she was alive that we were very good friends, I wouldn't doubt that she has told you of my misfortune, which you can end. I will tell you that God has just done me the favour of giving me as judges M. Amelot, minister of the department of the King's Household, and M. Le Noir, Councillor of State, lieutenant-general of police. They are two men of honour and integrity, fair and just. They deign to render me the justice due to me; but, as they are full of compassion, they would not want me, after twenty-eight years' captivity, to lack anything when I leave such a long prison term. Before releasing me, they would like to know if I have the necessary funds with which to support myself, or relatives who could lend me a helping hand. You're better informed than anyone else about my affairs, because it was your father or you who concluded the sales agreement for the house my mother bought from M. Bouliex, near the town square. You also know that she was well equipped with funds . . .'

And the letter continued on these pleasant lines suitable for great gentlemen . . . Danry was not to be surprised when he never received a reply, because the notary did not exist. But the lieutenant-general of police was to know of it, for the mail was censured. And first and foremost, before the letter was sent, it had been read to, and discussed at length by, the Chevalier de Moyria who was soon to be released. How could he not promise his support to such an unfortunate and kindly fellow prisoner, and when both of them were from Languedoc.

When the Chevalier left Charenton a few months later, Danry made him promise that he would stop in Montagnac before returning to Béziers. The reply was not fast in coming. Maître Caillet was probably dead. Like a gentleman, the Chevalier scrupulously performed this task, but in Montagnac, no one had ever heard of the Vicomte Masers de Latude or Maître Caillet. There had not been a notary in Montagnac for years.

The Chevalier did not doubt his companion's sincerity for one minute. Maître Caillet had probably died years ago. Twenty-eight years of captivity had dispersed the family and compromised the fortune of this unfortunate viscount, making a stranger of him in his own village. Arrived at last at his family in Béziers, a letter from Danry was already awaiting him. So what news did he have? Had Maître

Caillet sold or kept his mother's house? And Danry added with great perfidy that at times he wondered if down in Montagnac everyone he had known was not dead. Luckily, he still had a friend in whom he could put all his trust. 'Chevalier,' Danry concluded, 'you are the only one who can deliver me. Please ask your dear mother to write to M. Le Noir.'

The young man told his mother all about this unfortunate, who had been imprisoned for twenty-eight years, while his own six months of imprisonment had seemed an eternity to him. The letter was read by everyone in the family and all were deeply moved. Something had to be done for the Vicomte Masers de Latude. That same evening, Mme de Moyria took up her pen to write to an old friend of the family, Rear-Admiral Mercier de Saint-Vigor, comptroller-general of the Queen's Household.

Among the nobility, a letter of recommendation was gospel truth. A mere fifteen days later, at the beginning of June 1777, the lieutenant-general of police and a King's commissioner presented themselves at Charenton to listen to Masers. The superior came to tell Danry in paternal tones to prepare a short, good speech. He for his part told of the little house in Montagnac that his mother had willed to him. He wanted to go there to live out his last days in peace. He was past fifty-two, with such uncertain health that he certainly did not have many years to live. And then there was the Moyria family in Béziers which was willing to lend him assistance.

Le Noir listened attentively and, since the father superior only said nothing but good of him, the magistrate promised his freedom, provided however that it be in Montagnac and not in Paris. Danry promised and wanted to add something. The father superior then took him gently by the arm to remove him from the room, for fear that an indiscreet word would ruin what had been decided.

On 5 June 1777 Danry was set free by a *lettre de cachet* on the express condition that he immediately leave for Languedoc, forbidden to live in any other place, under any pretext whatsoever. Danry signed whatever they wanted. He was free now, legally free, for the first time in twenty-eight years.

Charenton was hardly out of sight behind the trees before Danry's state of exaltation gave place to one of worry and concern. These two years spent at Charenton had entirely divested him of what little money, and especially of the comfortable wardrobe that he had had upon arrival. Everything had been sold item by item to Saint-Bernard. When he bade a warm farewell to his kind friends, Danry had tried to borrow a little money from one or the other, especially from Saint-Bernard. As for his friend Saint-Luc, he had been transferred a month earlier to the Senlis Charity, after which his lunacy had worsened – for, as the father superior confided to Masers, who had been very upset by his departure, he was truly a madman, whose kind ways and pleasant company should not hide the fact that this high-ranking gentleman had killed a young woman from the village after sexually assaulting her.

When Danry asked for a loan from Saint-Bernard, the latter replied with embarrassment that he would need some form of guarantee. Had he any property in the world outside? Danry had replied: 'What do you mean? Have I any property?' Before the Marquise de Pompadour had had him sent to the Bastille his entire family had occupied positions of the highest order, and his mother had bequeathed to him a house and a sizeable amount of personal property. Saint-Bernard smiled sadly and said to him: 'My dear Masers, keep those tales for the minister. Here, everyone knows you don't have a penny to your name.'

And now Danry was on his way to Paris with just one pair of stockings. He had torn breeches with holes in them and no suit or hat. Instead of the good pair of custom-made shoes given to him at the Bastille, and which, like everything else, he had sold to buy wine and tobacco, he had nothing on his feet but a pair of old slippers that had been thrown away and given to him by the Charity friars. Last of all, this shabby outfit was completed by an old moth-eaten cloth frock coat purchased in Brussels in 1756.

How was it possible to obey the order of exile in these conditions, and with no money in his pocket? In Montagnac he would be considered a vagabond, or worse, a criminal returning from the galleys. No, Paris was really the only city in France where a man like him could make his way or at least get by. He was fifty-two and felt vigorous and strong. But first he had to find some money.

A friend of the Chevalier de Moyria, who lived on the Rue de Grenelle in the Gros-Caillou, could hardly believe that this strange person could have been sent by the Chevalier, for the latter was unusually nice in his choice of relationships. Nevertheless 25 *louis* were lent to Danry, who unhesitatingly signed a note 'guaranteed by his friend the Chevalier de Moyria.' It was more than he needed to buy new clothes and to rent a modest room in the same street, recommended by his generous broker.

The very next day, Danry went to the office of the lieutenant-general of police. After a long wait, the latter received him behind closed doors, advising him to obey the King's order and to leave for Montagnac without delay. Danry promised to. But he had barely left before he was forming a new plan. He would go to Versailles to thank M. de Saint-Vigor who, according to the police lieutenant, had played a decisive role in his release. After that, he would also have to thank the minister, M. Amelot, perhaps at the same time obtaining money for the journey. After

all, he still had a bonus coming to him for the projects he
had had adopted during the time he was at the Bastille.

However, Danry should have known that Versailles
would not bring him any luck. Despite all, there he was
again. After spending several days drafting petitions, he
waited upon M. de Saint-Vigor and M. Amelot, declaiming
and showing the copies of his plans to the other visitors.
Could neither one nor the other receive him today? That
need be no obstacle. Danry presented himself at the court
of the Prince de Beauvau of whom another person in the
waiting room had spoken highly. A short interview was
granted, during which Danry fawningly recounted his
misfortunes and proposed to write a memorandum which
His Highness would perhaps agree to transmit personally
to the King. Taken aback, the Prince de Beauvau promised
vaguely to do so, and then hurried to get rid of this man
with all his plans.

The following day Danry returned to Versailles, first to
present a long written statement at the Prince de Beauvau's
stately home. At M. de Saint-Vigor's, who was still
away, Danry delivered another memorandum in which he
demanded compensation, and lashed out insults at his
oppressors. He was then seen again visiting the minister of
the King's Household where he created a commotion in the
waiting room, taking aside a lady of respectable birth who
was awaiting an audience, showing her letters and even
going so far as to ask her in an almost threatening tone to
intervene on his behalf. The woman was offended. Attendants came to her rescue, roughly putting the troublemaker
outside. But the obstinate Danry still succeeded in giving
them his memorandum.

Once returned to his room on the Rue de Grenelle, Danry
felt that he had gone too far. Hadn't he, in his anger,
threatened the attendants who were showing him out that
he would have the memoranda he had written in prison

read in public. He remembered some remarks made by visitors about the severity of the minister. Wouldn't it be more prudent to leave Paris? But what would he do in Montagnac without money? His mother had died penniless, and no one would open the door to him. The whole situation would be different if he could arrive there with enough money to buy a small parcel of land or a business. No, it was quite impossible to leave like this without having interested some nobleman in his fate.

Several days passed as Danry feverishly wrote new memoranda, among which were a 'plan for preventing French soldiers from deserting, and a lengthy dissertation on the best way of achieving an abundancy of grain, entitled 'An Immortal Crown for Louis XVI'. These writings, together with new petitions addressed to the King, all the copies of his former writings, and in particular a manuscript comprising forty-one notebooks written in small hand-writing which related his memories, written at Vincennes and Charenton, were all stuffed into a big bag from which Danry could produce whatever document he needed with unfailing speed.

On 12 July Danry was back on the road to Versailles in a state of fury. No question of going to M. Amelot's or M. de Saint-Vigor's where the valets would certainly bar him from entering. He would, however, leave a letter at the entrance of M. Amelot's residence in which he would beg the minister to grant him at least a few hundred *livres* for his journey into exile.

But there remained the Prince de Beauvau who had extended him such a warm welcome the first time. When he arrived at his mansion, the Prince was just getting into his carriage. Danry rushed up, almost knocking the footmen over: 'Your Highness, were you able to give the King my memorandum?' 'But what are you doing here, sir?' replied the Prince de Beauvau. 'You are probably not aware that

M. Amelot was seized with fury when he learnt that you had made a scene at his home. He asked me not to send any of your writings on to the King or to anyone else. He also asked if I knew your address in Paris so as to have you arrested. In these circumstances, sir, you will understand that I cannot have anything more to do with you.' With these words the Prince stepped into his carriage, abandoning Danry, with the footmen staring at him and digging each other in the ribs.

This time Danry got the message. He immediately returned to Paris to collect his few possessions, and to leave the same evening on the horsedrawn barge at Auxerre. His landlord, who was also a native of Montagnac, accompanied him to the Seine. When the man returned to the Rue de Grenelle, the police were already there. In his last request to the minister, from whom he was asking a little money for the trip, Danry had written in large letters: 'Henri Masers de Latude, c/o Pierre Grollier, Rue de Grenelle in the Gros-Caillou'.

On 15 July Danry was in Saint–Bris, 43 miles from Paris, cursing his fate, counting over and over again the few *louïs* remaining in his pocket. A man dressed in black who had been observing him for some time, approached him politely: 'Sir, perhaps you are called Masers de Latude?'

'Viscount Masers de Latude,' Danry heedlessly agreed.

'Very good. I am police officer Marais and have come to arrest you in the name of the King.'

'Me, sir?'

'Yes, you sir.'

12

Hell at Bicêtre

With nearly 4,000 men locked up at the beginning of Louis XVI's reign, Bicêtre, for men, was, after the women's institution Salpêtrière, the second largest division of the general hospital of Paris set up in 1656. Indeed, owing to the lack of space in the provinces, Bicêtre had become the dumping ground for the entire kingdom. Every sort of contemporary distress was to be found there: old people and invalids, abandoned or sick children commonly referred to as the 'bad eggs', madmen, epileptics, people with scabs and pox. To these beneficiaries were added an important contingent of beggars who were not sick and prisoners placed by court order or by *lettre de cachet*.

These thousands of individuals had the common characteristic of being poor and not having anyone to support them. The community as a whole therefore assumed the burden of providing a minimum amount to the tune of 150 *livres* per annum. This was a far cry from the 600 *livres* paid for residence at Charenton and the 1,000 to 1,200 *livres* allocated by the King for his state prisoners at the Bastille or the castle-keep of Vincennes. The living conditions reflected this, that is to say that worse than Bicêtre could not be found. Commenting on the famous prison, Mercier was to write in his *Tableau of Paris*: 'This Bicêtre is a name impossible to pronounce without experiencing a feeling of repugnance, horror and contempt.'

In 1788 Mirabeau, after being locked up himself for a period in Vincennes, would give a vivid description of Bicêtre: 'We had the courage to go to Bicêtre; I say the courage, though I was not aware of all the horrors of this horrible encounter . . .' And Mirabeau went into particular detail on the underground dungeons, real tombs where total darkness reigned, but which, all things considered, were better than the main hall on the ground floor where 'vices were practised which the decency of modern times does not allow us to name . . .'

Danry was placed in one of the underground cells which were referred to as *cabanons*, or padded cells. This followed a short stay in the Petit-Châtelet prison where he had undergone lengthy interrogation. Had he not been to a lady of rank, inducing her with threats to lend him money? Did he intend having his memoirs, which had been seized from his person along with other documents, printed or made public? In any case he couldn't deny that he had been to Versailles several times and shown himself very importunate there. Finally, an inquiry conducted in Montagnac had just revealed that he was unknown there and that his mother, who had passed away many years before, had not left any estate.

Thus, arrested for the fifth time, a mere forty days after a release he had awaited for twenty-eight years, Danry was once again imprisoned. He was stripped of his clothes and told to put on a tattered shirt, a pair of rough homespun breeches, a sleeveless vest and a faded coat. This wretched costume was completed by a pair of clogs and a cap of the kind worn by galley slaves. Two soldiers armed with sticks then led him to an underground cell where the only sustenance given to him was bread and water.

In the padded cells of Bicêtre Danry was able to appreciate

its total contrast to the gentle captivity of Charenton, or even the Bastille or Vincennes. There all the prisoners were interesting, courteous people. Here, all the prisoners were uneducated, rude villains. As at Charenton, the prisoners could converse through the little windows in their cell doors. But what language! And what conversation! There were only degenerates, thieves and escapes from the galleys there, in short, all the scum of the earth.

In the evening, after the bread and water had been distributed, the little door-holes would be left open for an hour. Then the prisoners would poke their heads through these holes. They could see one another, talk to each other, give advice and tell each other about their greatest crimes. Very soon too they would curse each other, sometimes going so far as to throw empty bottles or clogs at one another. Then the sergeant of the guard would appear on the scene with a few *dindres* or 'scabs', recruited from among the prisoners themselves, who restored order by hitting with their sticks those not quick enough to pull their heads back in.

Once the little door-hole was closed again, there was almost complete darkness. There was nothing else to do but lie down on a foul pallet, the only piece of furniture he had in his tiny, windowless cell. The wooden walls gave off a foul smell of filth and urine, made even worse by the heat of the summer. The dark and damp made a perfect breeding ground for fleas and lice, which proliferated, literally eating the prisoners alive. They scratched themselves so much that they ended up with infected sores.

Bicêtre was divided into three distinct sets of buildings: one for the insane, one serving as a home and finally one where the prisoners were shut in. This last one had three main wards allocated to it: La Force, Saint-Léger and Fort-Mahon. The infirmaries were above these wards. Two other buildings, referred to as the 'new' and the 'old', held prisoners. They had padded cells underground and above ground instead of common rooms. Danry was finally placed in a permanent cell above ground in the new building. He was no longer seen as mad, but instead thought of as a dangerous recidivist and a deranged agitator.

The new cell was no better, but it had a dormer window which let in a little air and light. The usual fare was improved in principle solely through donations made by pious individuals. Twice daily what was politely called broth was poured over the black bread. On Mondays an ounce of salted rancid butter; on Fridays and Saturdays a few spoonfuls of peas from which a number of insects cooked with them had to be extracted; on Thursdays and Sundays, 2 ounces of dry, tough meat which was almost impossible to chew and which had to be swallowed after being bitten to pieces by their teeth. Only maddening hunger could bring them to swallow such an allowance of food, and Danry, who up until then had always been well fed, suffered terribly.

This was not even counting the hordes of fleas, which continued to devour him, despite the fact that he spent whole days killing them one at a time. Danry had had the idea of storing their remains in a little bag that he had made for this purpose. The speed with which the bag filled up brought tears of shame and despair to his eyes. Nevertheless, thanks to such evidence, he would be able to arouse righteous horror against his tyrants if he ever managed to extricate himself from this hell. Unfortunately, a guard discovered the bag of slaughtered fleas three months later in the course of a surprise inspection. 'This is really a mad idea!', were the disapproving words of the King's lieutenant when the gaoler had presented him with the strange, unsavoury object.

When winter arrived, damp and cold were added to the scene. With the first rains, water began to run down the walls, reviving the prisoner's rheumatism. The dormer window, with no glass in it, which two months earlier was a godsend in comparison with the pestilential underground cells, now let the cold wind and the first snow squalls blow into the cell. Soon it was as freezing as Siberia and Danry had to use his wooden shoe to break the ice in his water bucket.

Afflicted by rheumatism, the prisoner went whole days without getting up. His watchdog gave him no broth because he did not bring his bowl to the window in the door, and it was strictly forbidden to open the door. Only the bit of bread was thrown through the opening on to the bed where Danry lay, a prey to his sorrows.

At the end of the winter Danry could not even get up from his pallet. His legs were black and swollen.' His teeth, which chattered in extremely swollen, infected gums no longer allowed him to chew his bread. Seeing him always lying down and no longer eating his bread, the watchdog nevertheless deigned to become anxious. Someone came. Danry was dying of scurvy.

The surgeon had Danry transported on a stretcher to the Saint-Roch dormitory, which served as an infirmary. Extreme desolation reigned there: at one end were the victims of smallpox covered with cankers. They came from every correction centre in the kingdom, because Bicêtre was the only place where prisoners and criminals could be treated by rubbing and massive fumigation with mercury which led to the loss of hair and teeth and in some cases proved fatal.

The rest of the room was occupied by scurvy sufferers, of whom there were very many at Bicêtre. Their numbers were so great that there were not enough beds, and up to five or six patients were piled on to two beds side by side, with several mattresses thrown across them. The dying mingled with the convalescents under sheets that would have been in rags long before but for the filth and ointments smeared on to their bodies, which ended up hardening them.

As for the attendants, they were recruited from among the prisoners in exchange for a double portion of food. They did not rank any higher than the infirmary, spending more time stealing from the dead and dying than carrying out their tasks. Their job was otherwise limited and consisted essentially of giving food and drink to the sick.

Danry did not see the head surgeon until the day after his arrival. 'My friend,' he said to him, 'I'm going to cut away all that rotting flesh that is covering up your teeth.' Then, after the deployment of instruments of dubious sterility, the surgeon made a score of incisions in the mouth of the scurvy sufferer. He then took a pair of scissors and cut vigorously into the dead flesh covering the teeth and gums.

The cruel operation went on for fifteen days. The doctor would often cut into living flesh, and then blood flowed down, pouring over his chin and his chest. In the middle of all this, very hot plasters of ointment were placed on the sick man's legs, reputed to dissolve the coagulated blood in the scurvy sufferer's veins. Finally, the treatment was completed by making Danry swallow purges and herbal teas which he had to drink from a large cup which was passed from mouth to mouth without any thought of its being rinsed.

The sick man's stomach turned at the sight. All his senses revolted. He turned his head away in horror. But he was told that medicine was expensive and that nothing could be wasted. He had to drink from the cup whether he wanted to or not. He drank, sorry not to be dead. For six long months, he was to remain in this vile place.

After leaving the infirmary, Danry, still very weak, had been placed in a less unhealthy room than his previous cell, better lit, cleaner, with a view of the far countryside, and below of all the comings and goings through the royal courtyard. There the months went by. But Danry, clinging to life, did not despair, at fifty-five years old and although he had been locked up since the age of twenty-four, of regaining his freedom.

The bizarre species at Bicêtre came to his mind's eye. There were those, like him, who had been placed there by *lettre de cachet*, and then the old people, those who suffered from venereal disease, the mentally deranged who could sometimes be heard screaming in some faraway ward and yet again those who were detained by police or court order, who were identifiable by their infamous uniform, the black-and-white striped jacket and cap.

Those who had a little money could buy what they wanted or see an improvement in their daily fare. Anything could be bought, while the guards got rich on this sordid trade. Did a prisoner at Bicêtre want to write? They would sell him pens and paper. On the other hand, the guards and watchdogs were expressly forbidden, under pain of the most severe penalties, to deliver personal messages. Each morning, the head guard walked down the corridors shouting: 'Good morning, gentlemen.' These words were the signal for the collection of mail. Those who had some would knock on their partition and wait for the window in the door to be opened.

You had to remember then to pay a *sou*. That was the 'profit' charged by the guards, who otherwise would close the opening, pretending that they had not seen the letter waiting there. The mail collected thus was taken to the central office where it underwent merciless censorship, as did incoming letters. But special arrangements could be made with the powers on high, and the prisoners who offered several *livres* instead of a *sou* could get the most severe guard to turn into a zealous courier who would take messages himself concealed under his coat to Paris.

Danry observed all these goings on. Unfortunately he had nothing to offer his guards. The little remaining to him had been stolen at the infirmary along with a very pretty knife given to him by the Chevalier de Moyria at Charenton. It had a tortoiseshell handle inlaid with gold. Impossible therefore to purchase his guards' goodwill. But a large number of visitors came to Bicêtre every day to be shown over the place. Among them were people whose compassion and charity persuaded them to accept petitions which the prisoners surreptitiously smuggled to them.

Resolved to employ this method, Danry got a petition ready, awaiting only the arrival of a visitor whose attire indicated his or her importance. One day, he saw a lady who, he was informed, was a princess of the House of Bouillon. Several officers surrounded her with respect and showed her the institution's sad curiosities. As soon as the princess strayed a little from her retinue, the prisoners immediately threw petitions at her feet with consummate skill. With a knowing look, the great lady picked them all up and immediately hid them in her muff.

These actions, though forbidden, were part of the charm of the tour. After an expedition the visiting ladies liked to consider dangerous, they returned to the safety of their home to read the messages. Nevertheless, partly from a taste for intrigue and partly from compassion, some of them passed the messages on to their addressee who was more often an important person or a member of the Parliament of Paris who, it was hoped, would intervene.

When the princess went past his window, Danry in turn threw out his message. Unfortunately, the petition hit the shoulder of an officer before landing on the floor. He immediately picked it up and threw a furious look at the windows around him. Less than an hour later two guards came to fetch Danry from his cell to move him to a dungeon with no windows.

In May 1781, when Danry had been shut up in Bicêtre for nearly four years, many favours were granted on the occasion of the Dauphin's birth. A special committee, under the presidency of Cardinal Rohan and composed of eight advisors from Châtelet, came to gather at Bicêtre. Danry was heard with interest. He was even an object of sympathy. But the committee's decision was not favourable to him and furthermore, it was not empowered to suspend *lettres de cachet*. Danry, more than ever convinced that a universal conspiracy was set against him, wrote to the president of the Parliament of Paris: 'The foul breath of vice has never disheartened me; but there are magistrates who prefer to confer a favour by pardoning guilty men rather than exposing themselves to the deserved criticism that they committed the most revolting injustice by keeping an innocent man in chains for thirty-three years.'

In any case, the relative relaxation of the detention system, at a time when the great reforms of the realm had been set in motion in France's hospitals, hospices and detention centres, gave Danry the opportunity to resume his epistolary activity. Projects, memoranda and numerous writings on his misfortunes again bloomed under his fertile pen. There was, for example, a plan for a hydraulic press sent to the Marquis de Conglans, with the 'tribute from an unfortunate gentleman who has grown old in iron fetters'.

Danry often sold his bread ration, economizing *sou* by *sou* for weeks on end, to pay a gaoler to deliver his message to all those who could be concerned with his fate. So at the beginning of the 1780s his story was finally to be heard by a compassionate ear. France was reading Rousseau and shedding many tears, becoming the most sensitive nation in the world. This newborn romanticism, these 'surges from the heart' which Mme de Staël was to describe so well, were soon to take up Latude's story and his endless suffering.

It was first a priest from the parish of Saint-Roch, who was also a vicar at Bicêtre, who lent Danry a sympathetic ear. He came to see the prisoner, consoled him and gave him a little money. Cardinal de Rohan, before becoming interested in the Queen and seriously compromising himself in the Necklace Affair, showed interest in this prisoner who was beginning to become a household word in the salons. He even sent him help through his secretary.

Encouraged by this new contact, Danry wrote tirelessly from the depths of his cell, still despairing, as he began a seventh year of imprisonment at Bicêtre, of gaining his freedom one day. 'Yes,' he confided to whoever would read his writings, 'thirty-five years have gone by while I've languished in the harshest captivity. Time flies for people in the world outside, it drags for me . . . I live in a cell deep down, 10 feet underground; bread and water are my only food . . . Behold the tears that wet the pallet that serves as my bed.'

What he did not know, however, was that someone had already been actively working for the past two years to obtain his freedom . . .

13

Madame Legros

One day in the winter of 1781 a young woman found a package at the end of the Rue des Fossés-Saint-Germain-l'Auxerrois. The envelope had been destroyed by the damp, and the seal undone. She picked it up, opened it and looked for an address where she might be able to deliver the papers. Suddenly she felt a pang of anguish as she read the long signature: 'Masers de Latude, prisoner for thirty-two years at the Bastille, at Vincennes, and now at Bicêtre, on bread and water, in a cell 10 feet underground.'

A gaoler from Bicêtre who had been on his way to deliver this memorandum to a councillor of the Parliament had dropped it there one evening when he was drunk. The woman, who was a haberdasher by profession, called Madame Legros, went straight home to read the long tale of sufferings with her husband of this prisoner of the King. Their sensitive hearts were moved to indignation. The poor young man's innocence seemed so obvious to them that they swore that they would do all they could to get him out of there.

But it was Madame Legros who demonstrated tireless ardour, courage and devotion to the mission. Without relatives, friends, fortune or protection, she tried to arouse interest in the matter among high-ranking aristocrats and men in power. She went with the memorandum which she had copied several times before taking the original to its addressee. She spoke with 'that eloquence of spirit of which the mind is only the cold lie', Latude would later write in his Memoirs. People often listened to her and sometimes gave her hope. But what could be done against the King's will?

Madame Legros did not allow herself to be discouraged, increasing her visits, without fear of returning to the attack several times. 'What a great sight,' Michelet would write, 'to see this poor woman, badly dressed, going from door to door, paying court to valets to get into the great houses to plead her cause before great men . . .'

And now, after two years of exhausting effort, Madame Legros found the means of entering into contact with her protégé, with whom she could at last share her faith. Danry saw his benefactress for the first time. Tears were shed. A feeling of infinite tenderness was to bind the two individuals for the future . . .

'People of course wondered,' Bachaumont wrote in his *Secret Memoirs*, 'whether Madame Legros was pretty. These curious individuals would receive the reply that she was very ugly and that they should have guessed it because beauty and virtue rarely go together.'

Danry would henceforth be kept informed of Madame Legros's actions in every little detail, thanks to the carrying back and forth of messages by a very expensive gaoler. These tips, added to the money 'lent' to the prisoner at Bicêtre, and to the expenses of travelling around Paris and even to Versailles, where Madame Legros had gone several times to petition, were slowly ruining the household finances. Yet the Legros remained determined, and this despite the fact that Madame Legros had been told when she first went to Bicêtre 'that she was making a mistake by getting involved with a dangerous madman who before coming to Bicêtre had been confined at Charenton.'

At first perplexed, Madame Legros had not hesitated for very long. If M. de Latude was just another madman, why then had he not been left at Charenton, and why had he been treated so cruelly? She had once again read his memorandum, so often recopied, detecting in it the same profound humanity that she had been able to read in the prisoner's face. If M. de Latude had had a fit of madness in the past, it was because his detention had driven him to despair. But hope had dispelled all that.

Mme Legros therefore continued with her mission, completing the ruin of her household by obtaining the services of a parliamentary lawyer, M. Lacroix, and then a second one, M. Comeyras. At the same time, clear progress was made. New copies of the memorandum had been sent to better addresses, as the barristers had an extensive knowledge of names of people who could be petitioned in this sort of case. And this time, the doors opened much wider.

One day in autumn 1783, Le Noir, who was still lieutenant-general of police of Paris, went to Bicêtre to see Danry. He had sworn that he would never become involved with poison like that again, but now all of Paris was talking of nothing but 'M. de Latude'. It had become the sole topic of conversation. It was of course Le Noir who was portrayed, as usual, as the villain. His inspectors took great pleasure in what they considered their duty to report back to him on all the abusive remarks being spread about him. Hadn't he been paid a hefty bribe by the Comte de Maurepas, recalled from disgrace by Louis XVI and the real instigator behind the Affair of the Necklace, to keep a mere innocent accomplice in chains and to have more or less mistreated him to boot? And the fact that M. de

Maurepas had passed away some years before could only add fuel to this kind of slander.

This devil Danry would once again have pulled off one of those magical tricks, whose art he had perfected. No doubt at all that he was the one who had orchestrated this clique with libels and new lies. But today the matter had gone too far to be hushed up. The French Academy had been moved by the story and d'Alembert was all fire and fury because of it shortly before the occasion of his death that year.

In short, people had become infatuated with Latude as they had at the same time with Mesmer and with animal magnetism and as they would a few months later with M. de Beaumarchais's *Marriage of Figaro* – so many opportunities to slate those in power.

Le Noir no longer counted all the great men who mockingly stopped him in the corridors of Versailles to ask what great crime M. de Latude could have committed to deserve such a long imprisonment. Sometimes even hearing M. de Maurepas's name whispered behind his back was like a knife stabbing at his self-esteem. He was an honourable man, the son and grandson of highly esteemed magistrates.

For the ten years that he had been lieutenant-general of police he had devoted himself to transforming Paris into a modern city where 600,000 inhabitants might benefit not only from security, but also from health and a regular food supply. He had spent long days on inspection tours and entire nights awake in his office. It was he who had carried through the plan begun by Sartine to install lighting by street lamps, who had closed down the cemeteries inside the city walls, ordered the streets to be watered down, and imposed severe health regulations on butchers and knackers. It was also he who had organized the first fire brigade in Paris, instituted street numbering, set up a network of state pawnshops where a moderate, legal municipal rate of interest had at last been able to combat the scandal of private usury.

Le Noir would have preferred recognition for these actions, but all he saw around him was hate and political cliques. The only thing people associated with him were the Bastille and the *lettres de cachet*, giving him no credit for the enemies he had reconciled, the couples he had reunited, or the crimes he had prevented with a warning. There had certainly been some sort of change in the kingdom of France. People criticized the ministers, the police was loathed, and everywhere talk centred on reforms and the convening of the States General. Besides, Le Noir had decided to hand in his resignation as soon as the opportunity arose.

Dressed in a severe black velvet suit, set off with sparkling white lace, Le Noir was sadly going over all that in his mind as he sat at a rickety table in the 'best room' at Bicêtre. Behind him stood the institution's entire staff, eager to please him and waiting in silence. A sullen Le Noir sat cross-legged and swinging his legs, slowly caressing his shirt frill. He had had Danry brought in, and the prisoner also stood waiting to be addressed.

Le Noir pensively contemplated this nuisance who was earning him a bad reputation and, perhaps even more important, wasting his time. He had a hundred cases awaiting him. Now his office was flooded with requests for permission to visit this already famous prisoner at Bicêtre. The worst of it was that the requests were mostly from people of rank whom it was difficult to deny. Moreover, important men had already been seen coming to Bicêtre in their carriages without asking anything from anybody. With regard to this, Le Noir bitterly noted that he was no longer the first to be informed – this was surely too much for the lieutenant-general of police.

It was not, for example, until much later that he had

found out that the Marquis de Villette, who was one of the pillars of the Court, famous for his quarrels and also for his hospitality to the dying Voltaire, had sent his steward to Bicêtre, requesting the honour of rescuing 'M. de Latude.' This scoundrel Danry was to decline the offer, which nevertheless included a pension of 600 *livres*, replying that it would have been ungrateful on his part to deny Mme Legros the privilege!

And that was not all: Le Noir knew that this Mme Legros had managed to persuade Mme Necker to become involved in her cause, and he had been able to intercept a letter in which Danry called the minister's wife his Minerva. His Minerva! He also knew that one of the memoranda that had been circulating in Paris for the past two years had even been able to reach the Queen's cabinet. The Queen had been moved and had spoken of it to the King who had asked to see the case and had examined it carefully. That was why the day before, Le Noir had had to go with all speed to a meeting with His Majesty. Le Noir had come in person to deliver the King's reply to the prisoner.

An embarrassed cough finally brought the head of the Paris police force out of his morose meditation.

'Sir,' he said to Danry, 'you must surely be aware of all the commotion you have stirred up in Paris and at Court concerning yourself. What do you hope will come of it? Your freedom perhaps? But what else would you do if you were released than go to swell the crowd of those attacking the regime with their slanderous statements? What new folly would you get up to once at liberty?

'I'm an honest man, Sir, and I think I've earned the right, after thirty-five years of captivity, to spend the rest of my days now in peace with my benefactress. When are you going to grant me the freedom so many eminent people have been demanding for me?'

'Sir,' Le Noir sighed, 'I could scoff at you by replying

that I also met a most important person yesterday who spoke to me about your release. I want to stress the fact that I feel no hatred against you although your case has largely contributed to my being detested all over Paris. But I must tell you that I saw the King yesterday after the Queen had personally intervened on your behalf. His Majesty told me that you will never leave here.'

Nothing else could be said once the King had spoken. Even Mme Legros first bowed her head at the announcement of the terrible decision. But at Court everyone knew that Louis XVI was not an obstinate monarch. His severity towards Latude was even strange and could only be explained by the bad mood he had shown over all the ferment developing at Court over such a miserable affair.

So all hope was not lost. Mme Necker, this 'minister of charity', continued to intervene and the coming to power of the Baron de Breteuil, the Queen's man, was especially helpful in bringing about a dramatic turn of events. And indeed at the beginning of 1784 the new minister had a circular published reforming the *lettres de cachet*. These now had to be fixed for a specific period of time, thus avoiding abusively long detentions.

Yet Danry, whom everyone was calling Latude by now, had the longest record of detention of any prisoner in the whole of France. Only one other prisoner, the minister was informed after the archives had been consulted, had remained in prison for such a long period. This was Father De Ham, an Irish Jacobin, a dangerous madman imprisoned in the Bastille in 1686 following violent speeches against the King. In 1711, he had killed his gaoler by striking him with an iron bar from his bed. It was then decided that he would be shut up for life. His cell was condemned and his meals were served to him through a hole in his door. He died without religion in 1720 after remaining imprisoned in the Bastille for thirty-four years. He was buried in the garden.

No one would have thought of comparing Latude's case to such a serious affair. The minister finally managed to persuade the King to change his mind, and on 23 March 1784 Louis XVI grudgingly signed a *lettre de cachet* ordering the prisoner's release. There was already rejoicing, when it was suddenly realized that the King's order stipulated that he was to be exiled to Montagnac, even forbidding Latude to enter Paris, and insisting that he report upon arrival to the officer of the national police who was imperiously charged with the task of monitoring his behaviour. A pension of 400 *livres* would enable the exiled man to subsist rather meagrely of course, but, after all, that was to be expected for a former prisoner of the State.

Mme Legros personally came to deliver the order to Latude after Mme Necker had had it sent to her. The two friends wept in their despair. Would they have to part before even getting to know one another? No, it would be too unfair. So Mme Legros requested as a signal favour that her protégé should be kept at Bicêtre while she undertook new action. She and her husband personally volunteered to vouch for Latude's conduct. She saw Mme Necker again, begging her to intercede once more with M. de Breteuil. After a few days, the new *lettre de cachet* arrived, ordering release without restriction.

Nevertheless, there were implicit conditions which the hotheaded Latude would have been wise to keep in mind if he did not want to meet with yet another change in fate of the kind that had struck him so soon after his release from Charenton. It was Mme Necker in person who, although she refused to meet with Latude personally, reminded him of the fact in a letter:

'I was not the one, sir, who obtained your freedom; but I have taken a real interest in your misfortunes and have worked to convince all those people who, I felt, would be useful to you. . . . I recommend to you therefore to be silent on your past misfortunes; forget all those whom you believed to be your enemies; make this sacrifice to God, to your protectors, and especially to your future safety which depends absolutely on your good behaviour. There is no one in the world to whom you owe as much as to Mme Legros. . . . The slightest carelessness on your part would redound upon her . . .'

14

Vicomte de Latude, Pensioner of the King

Notwithstanding this kind warning that Latude (we shall call him that from now on) would not forget, a favourable period began for the man who had become the hero of all Paris. Despite his fifty-nine years and his rheumatism, which was the least to be expected after almost an entire life in the King's prisons, Latude had retained an alluring youthfulness and a lively spirit, which drew the admiration of all those who met him, and they were many. His name was in fact on everyone's lips. He was fêted everywhere and everyone was sorry for him, readily comparing him with Robinson Crusoe whose story had only recently come into fashion thanks to Jean-Jacques Rousseau. A surprising coincidence: hadn't it also taken Robinson thirty-five years to return to his own kind.

The Robinson of the prisons now lived in a modest, but clean and comfortable apartment not far from his benefactors who pampered him as if he were their own son. Despite the four floors and the narrow staircase, there was a constant coming and going of visitors, and especially of female visitors, who brought the unfortunate man not only their tears, but also some financial help. Marquises, magistrates, men of letters and sometimes some great Spanish nobleman passing through Paris flocked to see the man who now went by the name of 'Viscount de Latude, Pensioner of the King'.

At times there were so many people in the tiny flat that the door had to be left open so that those packed on the staircase could hear Latude speak. Over and over again, with unrelenting complacency, he told the terrible story of his captivity, while in the street the sound of horses and carriages could be heard. An amazing sight to see these duchesses and marquises on the staircase barring the way with their magnificent robes of the visitors going out after leaving a coin, which Latude discreetly called 'a sign of their sensitivity' on the end of a table. People apologized, pushed, laughed. In the salons in the evening, a lady who had not paid a visit to the Vicomte de Latude was not keeping up with the times. It was also unfashionable for a lady never to have been to M. Mesmer's tub. But she would promise, she would go tomorrow.

Latude did not content himself with his own sitting-room, gladly accepting invitations to dinner. A hostess who had received the Vicomte de Latude at her table was sure to be famous for several months, something not to be underestimated in Paris. People also fought over the man of the day for whom these animated dinner parties were a fine revenge for thirty-five years of injustice. It was a marvel to see him eat and drink for four and at the same time answering with his Gascon joviality, the thousands of questions fired at him.

When everyone moved to the sitting-room, a respectful silence would suddenly fall. M. de Latude, seated in a gold-coloured armchair in front of a blazing fire, would prepare to tell his story. The women would huddle around him, forming a multicoloured, rustling bouquet with their dresses. The time had come to drop a gentle tear. When M. de Latude had finished speaking, chocolate would be served.

A person's poverty did not diminish if he became a pensioner of the King and only received 400 *livres*. But there were many rich visitors who did not content themselves with just leaving a mere 100 *livres* on their departure. Latude soon received 500 *livres* a year from President Dupaty and 300 *livres* from the Duc d'Ayen. Furthermore, a public subscription had been opened, in which almost all the greatest names participated: the Maréchales de Luxembourg and de Beauvau, the Duchesse de la Rochefoucauld, the Comtesse de Guimont, the Marquis de Villette, the Chevalier de Pougens, son of the Prince de Conti.

Mme Legros, who had been financially ruined during these years by all she had done, was not forgotten. In its session of 25 August 1784, the French Academy had decided to award Mme Legros the annual prize for virtue which had been founded two years earlier by the Baron de Montyon for 'the poor Frenchman who has accomplished the most virtuous action'. Marmontel, a famous author throughout Europe, a member of the Academy since 1763, who had had an introduction to the Bastille in 1759 while editing *Le Mercure de France* had delivered the following speech: 'It is in the presence of virtue crowned with glory that the Academy has the satisfaction of awarding this prize to an obscure woman whose constant, disinterested care has for two years overcome the greatest obstacles to extricate an unfortunate man from the most miserable situation . . .' With her usual modesty, Mme Legros was present to receive the prize to the acclamation of the entire assembly. This was a gold medal, which she was forced to sell almost at once because of her extreme poverty.

This sad detail violently moved Latude's benefactors, and on 12 May 1786 they managed to secure an annual pension of 600 *livres* for Mme Legros from the comptroller-general of finances, M. de Calonne, to be paid out of funds used to help gentlefolk fallen into misery. The minister's letter even stipulated that this assistance was granted on behalf of the King to Mme Legros 'after she had sacrificed herself to help M. Le Vicomte de Latude, detained for so many years at Vincennes and recognized as innocent.'

Shortly after this, the Duchess of Kingston also arranged for another pension of 600 *livres*. Now the Legros and their adopted son were assured a comfortable life. But it was not too much when you thought of the debts contracted by the Legros, which had to be reimbursed. It was not even enough for Latude whose immoderate ambitions exceeded his rank in life.

But, as La Fontaine so rightly says, 'all stability comes late and lasts a short time'. In 1788, after several years of unquestionable fame and brilliant living, Latude realized that infatuation for his person since his release would not last for ever. Already he was receiving fewer invitations, and conversations in the salons had turned to the War of Independence in the United States of America and especially to the convening of the States General. His story had taken second place.

Latude could nevertheless content himself with the several pensions that had been granted to him and combined to make a nice sum. But now the incorrigible Gascon was possessed again by his old demons. Well then? Should he have to be content with a meagre 2,000 *livres*' annual income when the Crown had made millions, thanks to his reform projects which had almost all been carried out. Besides, this would be to hold cheap a whole life spent in prison for an unjust motive. Come along, all hope of becoming rich was not lost.

His first objective would be to keep Parisians, who were a forgetful lot by nature, informed of his story by other

means than conversations in the salons. And since the
publication of his Memoirs, with the risk of a return to the
Bastille, was out of the question, why not put on a play
and court public favour, ever eager for topical subjects? In
fact, two theatres had just been closed on the Boulevard du
Temple. M. Legros was easily persuaded to become a
partner in this undertaking. All that remained to be done
was request a thirty-year privilege from the King.

Latude was not sufficiently naïve to believe that the
lieutenant-general of police, chief censor of the orthodoxy
of plays (and of the private life of actresses), would take a
favourable view of his story being played in public, especially
since emotion was at its height with the announcement of
the convening of the States General. So the letter he
addressed to the King was totally discreet as to the nature
of the performance he wanted to put on. 'Sire,' he wrote,
'if the unfortunate are entitled to kindness of heart . . . On
the Boulevard du Temple, intrigue, jealousy and greed have
succeeded in closing down two theatres. One is that of
opera trainees and the other that for light comedy. Now,
I beseech Your Majesty to be so kind as to bestow on me
the same privilege . . . of organizing one of these two
shows, or another one . . .'

Although Latude promised an annual donation of a 1,000
écus for hospitals and another 1,000 in support of the opera,
recalled that his misfortunes 'entitled him to the favour he
was asking' and ended by claiming to have originated the
reforms for the arming of non-commissioned officers and
for contracts for the postal system, that 'or another one'
did not fail to raise a smile in Le Noir's successor, who
refused permission. Why didn't he ask for a guided tour of
the Bastille while he was at it?

On 26 August 1788 the Duchess of Kingston died. She
was an extremely rich Englishwoman who had moved to
Paris in 1788 and had linked up with all in high society,

and with the literary and theatrical world. Her unusually eventful life had always been the talk of the town. This woman, who was nevertheless an excellent character, gladly helped out the unfortunate and had some years before given a pension to Mme Legros.

When her death was announced, Latude was full of excitement, convinced that the eccentric millionairess would not have forgotten him in her will. He rushed to collect his share, he assumed an important air, but there was nothing for him. It was a bit too much! Letters flowed in abundance, raging and threatening. Even the Marquis de Villette, with whom only the day before the Vicomte de Latude had shared open house, received a very unpleasant letter (yes, from this man who was increasingly being considered a nuisance).

On 22 November 1788, when the Duchess of Kingston's furniture and belongings were sold on the Boulevard Saint-Martin next to the Opera House, Latude was there in full view saying that he was a legatee of the Duchess, and even buying a few objects which he paid for with a gold *louis*. The sale resumed in the afternoon and the Vicomte de Latude was there again, his wig carefully powdered, ready to enter.

But what was happening? An usher barred his way, explaining in a low voice that he had express orders not to let him enter. Latude forced his way in and started speaking in a loud voice. By what right could they deny entry to the Vicomte de Latude, who had been honoured by the kindness of the late Duchess?

'You see, sir,' the auctioneer's usher replied, embarrassed by the scandal under way, 'you paid us with a worthless *louis* this morning.'

'Worthless? You mean to imply perhaps that my *louis* was false? I demand an apology and order you to let me enter!'

'And I, Sir, beg you to leave!'

'Insolent man! They've put a rogue on the door, and not a gentleman . . .'

The row continued to such a point that the exasperated usher had the mounted police sent for. Latude was ignominiously thrown out in the street before a laughing crowd, trying to maintain his calm and dignity. On the same day, Latude would file a complaint against the usher for slander 'prejudicial to his honour and reputation', with a demand for reparation. The complaint, filed with the tribunal of Châtelet, was to come to nothing. Paris had certainly become too ungrateful and it was time to leave for other climes . . .

England, which had the inconvenience of an equally detestable climate and food, did, however, have the considerable advantage of placing Latude beyond the reach of the French police. Since seduction no longer worked for him, our hero decided to bring legal action against Sartine, Le Noir and even Mme de Pompadour's heirs. Faced with such adversaries, it would be wiser to write memoranda and petitions sheltered from any mischance.

The first memorandum against M. de Sartine whom Latude considered to be chiefly responsible for his detention in that hell, informed the former lieutenant-general of the Paris police of the conditions under which the plaintiff would refrain from legal action: 'M. de Sartine, will you give me, in the form of redress for all the evil and damage that you have caused me to suffer unjustly, the sum of 900,000 *livres*.' Another memorandum demanded 600,000 *livres* from M. Le Noir, and a third 100,000 *écus* from the Marquise de Pompadour's heirs. Together, the three sums totalled 1,800,000 *livres*, that is, enough to put the person who had that much money among the ten or fifteen wealthiest people in Paris.

Latude had been in England for a few months and was

beginning to realize that it would be difficult for him to remain in exile if his legal actions did not succeed, when he learned that the meeting of the States General at Versailles on 5 May 1789 had finally degenerated into a revolt. On 17 June the deputies of the Third Estate proclaimed themselves the National Assembly. These were the first mutterings of revolution. Hastily, Latude left for Paris where for sure fortune would finally smile on him.

15

Citizen Latude, Victim of Despotism

In an increasingly agitated Paris at the beginning of that summer of 1789, Latude was as happy as a sandboy. Everywhere around him people were talking about constitution and liberties. A city council had been set up at the Town Hall while people in the streets spoke of arming themselves quickly to resist the groups of soldiers that Versailles was concentrating around Paris. Latude, who no longer had to fear reprisals in such an atmosphere, had already begun to draft part of his Memoirs. Hastening to dispose of his false title and wig, he was henceforth the person who had suffered from despotism all his life. Besides, through his escapes, hadn't he resisted tyranny at the risk of his life?

And then suddenly, on 12 July, the insurrection exploded, beginning in the gardens of the Palais-Royal where speakers such as Camille Desmoulins had been haranguing the crowd for weeks. At sixty-four, Latude was no longer of an age to run through the streets, and still less carry a gun, but he kept a close watch on events. So what were his feelings when he heard of the attack, and then the capture, of the Bastille!

From the day after that memorable event, Latude, in the role of an ardent patriot, presented himself at the famous citadel which was in process of destruction. Despite orders not to let anyone in, Latude insisted, stating his name and recalling his long period of captivity. The 'Conquerors of the Bastille' then acclaimed him, only too happy to find in this exemplary prisoner an additional justification for the piteous massacre of a garrison as it surrendered.

His name was already on everyone's lips when, in a highly emotional state, he penetrated the loathsome wall. He first asked to be taken to the top of the towers, a pilgrimage that had been accomplished three years earlier by a spry old man of ninety who had been 'sentenced to the Bastille' several times in his life: the Duc de Richelieu, great-nephew of the famous Cardinal. However, Latude did not contemplate his past from the top of the towers, but his future. It was not the time for recollections, but for answering the questions being fired at him amid the noise from the excited crowd of patriots busy demolishing some of the battlements.

Yes, of course it was he, Latude, who had spent much of his life there because of the hatred of the Marquise de Pompadour. He had escaped from the Bastille one night in the winter of 1756 from this very tower. And now here he was, retracing the path in reverse, pointing out the chimney, telling of his fellow escapee who had died insane. His hearers were stirred with emotion. What a revenge for Latude.

He was followed right to the cell from which he had escaped. But where was the rope ladder that made the escape possible? Everyone was ready to believe the former prisoner, but pulling off such a miracle seemed virtually impossible. Latude insisted, was led as far as the Archives Room which had already been pillaged. He searched at length. A trap door was discovered in the ceiling which Latude wanted to open. But what were they to think? Perhaps there were other prisoners there (only seven prisoners had been freed from the whole Bastille the day before) or even hidden soldiers? French guards were summoned, arriving armed to the teeth. The trap door was forced. The men positioned their weapons. But the false ceiling only turned out to contain several sacks of miscellaneous objects and, among them, the rope ladder and wooden ladders that had been used for the escape, along with a number of documents about the prisoner . . .

Latude and his effects were carried off with the same enthusiastic spirit to the Town Hall. Once again, he was asked to tell the story of his escape which was henceforth about to become famous. In the end, ladders and documents were given to him as 'things belonging to him for all sorts of reasons'. The gentlemen suggested, however, that he should display them and no longer waste time before writing his Memoirs which would enlighten the people. Meanwhile, Latude proposed that they should come to see him at his home whenever they pleased. He lived at the Maison de Théatins on the Rue de Bourbon, no. 36.

Latude's home no longer received visits from ladies of leisure, but from patriots. Antoine Vestier, a painter at the Royal Academy, came to do a half-length portrait of him. In it Latude stares out proudly at posterity, one hand on his famous rope ladder, while with the other he points to the Bastille as it is being torn down stone by stone. The portrait was displayed at the autumn exhibition of 1789 where it met with enormous success. Engravings soon followed. At the bottom of one of the engravings, the following lines were etched:

> Instruit par ses malheurs et sa captivité,
> A vaincre des tyrans les effort et la rage,
> Il apprit aux Français comment le vrai courage
> Peut conquérir la liberté.

> (Taught by his misfortunes and captivity,

To triumph over tyrants' effort and rage,
He showed Frenchmen how true courage
Can conquer freedom.)

Another one read:

Victime d'un pouvoir injuste et criminel
Masers dans les cachots eût terminé sa vie
Si l'art du despotisme aussi fier que cruel
Avait pu dans ses fers enchaîner son génie.

(Victim of an unjust and criminal power
Masers would have lived out his last days in the cells
If the art of despotism both cruel and proud
Could have shackled his genius in its chains.)

After fostering such awareness amongst the public, all that
remained was the formidable multiplying effect of his
writings which had contributed as much to Latude's fame
as the conversations of the salon. Latude realized that he
had to act quickly. So in this feverish atmosphere he wrote
two short works which appeared just at the end of 1789.
The first, *Mémoire de M. Delatude, ingénieur* (Memoir of
M. Delatude, engineer), was sold for the modest price of
12 *sous* and told of his escape from the Bastille – which was
unquestionably his greatest claim to glory. The second
work, which Latude had based on the documents he had
recovered during his visit to the Bastille noted above, was
a reproduction of the long memorandum he had addressed
to the Marquise de Pompadour, along with several letters
addressed for the most part to M. de Sartine, lieutenant-
general of police.

Several clandestine apocryphal accounts of his adventures
had already appeared in 1789 and had only received a limited
audience despite, or because of, their political intentions

('the facts contained in this report', one read, 'are, so to say, proof of the awful despotism devastating France, of which the Comte de Mirabeau complains with such energy in his marvellous work, *Lettres de Cachet and the State Prisons*').

Latude took the opportunity in his first writings of repudiating these editions and of recalling that the facts recounted there seemed so incredible that everyone had believed that it was a work of imagination. It was also to avoid the appearance of the same disbelief that Latude managed to have his rope ladder and the other instruments used for the escape from the Bastille displayed at the entrance of a room in the Louvre. His painted portrait was also there for all to see, as were his first works in which he announced the forthcoming publication of his Memoirs.

By the end of this year 1789, when the King and the National Assembly had been set up in Paris, Latude no longer referred to royal despotism, but to 'the cruelest excesses of ministerial despotism'. With the same caution and also because he was rightly wary of his style and spelling, Latude preferred to entrust the drafting of his Memoirs to a professional writer whose pen could turn his sad adventures to good account. A young lawyer from the Nancy bar association, whose name was Thiéry, was chosen on the advice of the Chevalier de Pougens, a former benefactor and now a friend of Latude.

Between two sessions of intensive work, during which the attorney Thiéry had difficulty in putting the flood of memories and comments of his model into order, Latude resumed his letter-writing as feverishly as ever: at first these were floods of memoranda in a vengeful tone against the former lieutenant-general of police, Le Noir and especially Sartine ('Between the two of us, M. de Sartine . . . you deserve to be strangled with Le Noir's guts . . .'). The sums demanded by way of damages (1,800,000 *livres* alone from Sartine) were incredible. Anticipating those who might object that this was too much, Latude developed the argument that it was the best way to punish a man well known for his appetite for money and for his greed.

Dozens of letters were also sent to all the prominent people of the day to announce the forthcoming publication of his Memoirs. So, on 16 February 1790 Latude wrote to the patriot Palloy who since 15 July 1789 had been overseeing the costly destruction of the Bastille by a crew of 600 workers. It was Palloy who had had the bright idea of distributing little Bastilles sculpted from stones taken from the demolition to the chief towns of the new French departments. Fame, more than fortune, had been his driving force. 'I was there at the Bastille', Latude wrote to him, 'the day after its capture, and I saw the walls I had covered for so long with my tears; I felt totally different when I saw those bolts that free hands had just broken, which for so many centuries had always ruthlessly kept oppressed innocence locked up . . .'

Le despotisme dévoilé ou Mémoires de Henri Masers de Latude, détenu pendant trente-cinq ans dans diverses prisons d'État (*Despotism unveiled or the Memoirs of Henri Masers de Latude, detained for thirty-five years in various State prisons*), dedicated to La Fayette, appeared in the spring of 1790, and met with enormous success. In 1793, twenty editions would have been exhausted and the work translated into several languages. The *Mercure de France* would later write that henceforth it was the duty of parents to teach their children to read from this sublime work.

By dictating to Thiéry the very dressed–up story of his life (he was born a noble; he met the Marquise de Pompadour at Versailles and she offered him a purse full of gold which he refused; he had been behind the entire escape plan at the

Bastille; etc.), Latude established his own legend gloriously. A failed swindler, but a successful martyr, he had been able to combine at one stroke the interest of a political document (he referred to himself at that time as 'the most celebrated victim of despotism') with that of a shattering story capable of touching sensitive souls. 'The true story of my life is no more than that of misfortunes,' he wrote, with good reason.

The publication of Latude's Memoirs soon took on an official character with the speech Thiéry was to give to the bar of the National Assembly on 7 May 1790. To reach the Salle du Manège where the Assembly sat, one had to pass through the Tuileries gardens. In the spring these paths and these benches took Latude back half a century to when in that same place he had conceived the crazy project which was to cost him so dear. Not far from there, the bench where two strollers had spoken so violently against the Marquise de Pompadour. This unplanned pilgrimage moved him even more perhaps than the one he had accomplished the previous year at the Bastille. He felt dizzy and sat down and cried, while his attorney grew impatient.

Lawyers possess the art of exploiting the most unexpected situations. Demanding 'the religious respect that the Ancients had for a tree struck down by lightning', Thiéry explained that 'M. Latude had left him with the task of addressing you since the weakening of his organs and the emotion he feels in your presence does not allow him to address you.' Having said that, Thiéry announced to the deputies of the National Assembly that the public story of thirty-five years of misfortune was presented that day 'on the altar of the homeland'. Thanks to these Memoirs, the people would know better, *a contrario*, the price of the benefits with which their representatives were henceforth providing them.

The Assembly loudly applauded this speech, to which the president replied: 'Sir, you have acquired the unhappy fame of misfortune for a long time now.' Tribute was paid in passing to Mme Legros who had known how well to 'replace the care of Providence'. As for Latude, he was the first to dare to undermine 'the foundations of those horrible dungeons'. But, the president added nevertheless, it would not be possible to accuse the 'good, humane monarch who governs us'. It was 'without his knowledge' that these misfortunes afflicted the prisoner and 'he set them right as soon as he got to know of them.'

These speeches were printed soon after and contributed greatly to the success of the Memoirs. But the collaboration between Latude and Thiéry was not to continue. Paid a lump sum of 400 *livres* for the composition of the work, Thiéry, who could see the number of printings rapidly disappearing, understandably felt wronged. He asked for more. Latude, whose dreams of becoming rich were only equalled by his meanness, categorically refused. This was the break, each claiming to put out by himself a new edition of the Memoirs. Latude then let it be known that his own copies would henceforth be illustrated by his portrait and signed personally ('to avoid forgery').

Encouraged by the success of his book and the favourable welcome paid to him by the National Assembly, Latude soon began to claim a pension, asking to be treated as a 'victim of the State'. In a petition dated 21 May 1790, he catalogued his misfortunes in detail and requested an increase in the meagre pension of 400 *livres* granted to him since his release in 1784, which he had been receiving only on an irregular basis since the meeting of the States General.

Thirty-five years of captivity, 135 months of them in awful dungeons, deprived for nineteen years of fire and light, seven years on bread and water and for forty whole months without a single moment of respite with hands and feet in chains, lying on a bed of straw, with no blankets, so many insults, so many humiliations,

so many sighs and so many tears, will undoubtedly
arouse the greatest interest in the paternal heart of the
representatives of the most generous of all nations.

In 1791 Latude repeated his request for a pension, which
was finally refused in the course of an offensive speech by
the deputy Voidel demanding whether 'a generous nation
should encourage base behaviour such as that of which
M. Latude is guilty', pointing out also that the petitioner
had already obtained 'means of subsistence from several
individuals', and finally regretting that 'so much time has
already been wasted on this subject.' In the same spirit, the
Constituent Assembly voted in favour of discontinuing the
pension granted by the King in 1784. It should be said that
in a year of serious financial crisis and political toughening,
it was a bad moment to ask for pensions.

But Latude would have no regard for such considerations.
He fired up: 'What madness has taken hold of the minds
of the representatives of the most generous nation in the
universe! . . . To assassinate a poor man whose appearance
alone arouses pity and excites the least expansive sensitivity
. . . for death is not as terrible as the loss of honour!'

Fortunately for him, the Legislative Assembly which met
on 1 October 1791 was composed of completely new
deputies, the Constituent Assembly having decided, before
separating, that none of its members would be eligible for
the new assembly. With much persistence therefore, Latude
was personally admitted before a new audience on 26 January
1792. He had Mme Legros brought there, and to make the
show complete, he brought his ladder ('this curious object
which will never cease to arouse amazement in sensible
people', he noted). He revealed that for the past eight years
he had been living on nothing but loans and that at the age
of sixty-eight, after forty-two years(?) of detention he was
no longer in a state to work.

On 25 February 1792 a 3,000-*livre* pension was granted after the deputy Lasource had made a speech in direct opposition to Voidel's, a year earlier: 'When tyranny came down with its heavy hand on this unfortunate man, he used his own blood to draw a plan he had conceived in his cell to increase the national force . . . His cause is that of innocence; his advocate is humanity . . .'

Why stop when everything was going so well? Latude then turned against the heirs of Mme de Pompadour and against the former minister Amelot, bringing his case before the Court of the Sixth District of Paris and requesting damages and interest for his arbitrary detention and the abusive prolongation of his imprisonment. Public opinion was soon enthralled in this lawsuit which was in fact far from the ordinary.

The judgment passed on 11 September 1793, as well as the considerations on which it was based, were even less ordinary. In order to put the responsibility for Latude's martyrdom upon Mme de Pompadour and her heirs, the judges began by evading the argument according to which it could not be proven in any way whatsoever that it was in fact the Marquise de Pompadour who had prolonged his detention. 'There is no doubt of it on the one hand,' they replied, 'because exercising absolute power over the mind and heart of Louis XV, when the Pompadour wanted something, she only had to speak, not, like the others, being obliged to present memoranda, and on the other hand, because if she had wanted to end the evils of Latude's captivity, which she unquestionably knew about in all its details, all that she would have had to do was ask her lover for the release of this poor man. The King, so irritated by Latude's escapes from the Bastille and Vincennes, as might be supposed, was too weak to resist the desires, still less the caresses, of this siren.'

But was this a reason to accuse the Pompadour's heirs?

Beginning with the sole statement that Latude's detention was prolonged thirteen years beyond the death of the favourite, the judges were of the opinion that it was 'legitimate to think that the wicked woman's relatives had inherited her vengeful spirit in addition to the immense property that she had stolen from France, and rightly fearing problems from Latude whose ardent genius and impetuous nature were known to them, it was the Pompadour's relatives who, during the remaining years of Louis XV's life, had exercised all the credit that they had in a corrupt Court to remove from this unfortunate man the very possibility of making a claim against the unbelievable humiliation inflicted upon him . . .'

Here was Latude's thesis on the conspiracy of sorcerers and the magician Pompadour almost entirely sanctioned! Whatever the case, Latude ('quite well known for his misfortunes during the *ancien régime*', *Le Moniteur* wrote) still managed to win 60,000 *livres* in damages with interest (40,000 against the dame de La Gaillissonnière, heiress to the Pompadour, and 20,000 against Amelot). The sum of 10,000 *livres* was granted by way of provision, and the remainder was to be paid in good farmland of the Beauce.

Better still, when the property that had belonged to the Marquise de Pompadour was sequestered following the emigration of certain members of her family, Latude was to succeed in having his farmland put into his possession by the Directory of the Department of the Loir-et-Cher. And when the Pompadour heirs attempted in 1797 to have the ruling overturned, pronounced as it was under the Terror, the request would be rejected, the Executive Directory judging that Latude 'was justified in demanding what was legitimately due him from the Republic, and that his misfortunes, his advanced age and his pitiful position gave him after all rights to the government's goodwill . . .'

Others would follow Latude's example and obtain compensation with interest from former ministers, and even against their successors or their heirs. This would be so in the case, for instance, of Jean-Charles-Guillaume Le Prévôt, otherwise known as de Beaumont, who in 1794 obtained 450,000 *livres* in damages with interest from Bertin and Amelot, and from the estates of Laverdy, Sartine, Le Noir, Breteuil and Malesherbes, for having been arbitrarily detained for more than twenty-two years in the Bastille and in other prisons, for seditious memoranda.

However, in order to be a citizen, and not among the lesser ones, Latude still concealed a secret wound: that of his illegitimate birth, that of being basically, despite the fame of Latude, simply Jean-Henri, son of Jeannette Aubrespy and an unknown father. So in his *naïveté*, he sent a request in 1792 to one of the legitimate sons of the late Henri de Vissec de Latude asking him to recognize him as his natural brother. The latter did not even consider it worth replying.

During that same year, however, Latude glowed with his last official recognition when a donation was made to him by the Council of the Commune of Paris. The equestrian statue of Louis XV in ancient dress had been knocked down on 11 August 1792 on the Place de la Révolution, or what was soon to become the Place de la Concorde. Only the right hand had been recovered, and it was this hand that was solemnly offered to Latude, who would have certainly preferred some additional cash bonus. He could not understand that, as a living and already irrelevant symbol of royal despotism, it was with symbols that he was to be paid.

16

The Final Years

At the end of 1799, when the Directory was in agony and
Bonaparte, returned from Egypt without his army, was
preparing to carry out the coup d'état that would turn the
final page in the history of the French Revolution, Latude
attempted in these difficult times some writings on issues
of the time. First there was a 'memorandum on ways of
restoring public credit and order in the finances of France,
by citizen Latude, author of the historical Memoirs on his
life, his detention for thirty-five years in various State
prisons'. If its design was confused and not very convincing,
nevertheless an original, dangerous idea was put forward
in this little work: every landowner should set his own
taxes.

   Another work by Latude appeared the same year under
the title of 'Proposal for a coalition of 83 departments in
France to save the Republic in less than three months'.
Latude threw billions into it freely, returning also to the
issue of landowners which was dear to his heart since he
had won his farmland in Beauce. The whole work was as
obscure as the preceding one – as the author himself
confessed at the conclusion: 'I may not have expressed
myself very clearly . . .'

   Nearing seventy-five, Latude increasingly tended to
ramble on, having difficulty in accepting the fact that he

was no longer recognized so often in the street, and that his Memoirs, continually re-edited until then, were no longer selling so well. More than the tremendous thirst for money (which in his case was no small matter), there was that for reputation. Latude suffered from the fact that he was no longer the public man, the hero he had been during the years following the capture of the Bastille. Yet an impressario had taken his rope ladder on tours for several years through all the towns in France and even to England. Latude had even entered upon a correspondence on this subject with a lord who had come shortly after the capture of the Bastille to look at his ladder ('like all sensible people, you tell me that this work was worthy of curiosity'). But by now he no longer enjoyed outright fame. The war and the bloody consequences of the Revolution were much more powerful subjects.

Nevertheless, Latude spent his time sustaining his renown, not hesitating to write to famous people, and even to several sovereigns in Europe. For instance, here he is, writing to the King of Spain, even sending him his portrait and a copy of his Memoirs: 'O Prince, all human beings seek happiness and I would have found it if Your Highness deigned to receive my portrait with favour and the memoir of my three escapes from the tower of Vincennes and the Bastille, and at the same time give support with your powerful protection to the same homage that I take the respectful liberty of paying to the most virtuous and wisest of all rulers, the King of Spain . . .'

There followed a morass of statements returning again to the 'reform of spontoons and halberds', which Latude after so many years continued to claim as his invention for the benefit of the French army and now for the Spanish army. Was it compensation, or at least some token of thanks that Latude was seeking? He let the monarch be the judge of that, contenting himself with writing that 'it was

just and fair that his Majesty should deign to wipe away
with his paternal hands the tears of a poor father . . .' (the
child being the famous reform).

Letters of the same kind, again accompanied by a volume
of his Memoirs and a portrait, were addressed to the
Archduke Charles, brother of the Emperor of Germany, to
the King of Sweden, to the King of Denmark, to Jefferson,
President of the United States, not to mention, of course,
Bonaparte himself. The Revolution was hardly dead and
buried before he had hailed him as a saviour. And when
Bonaparte was to become Napoleon, he bowed before the
Emperor, but without denying himself the pleasure of
outlining for him, in a long letter, the lines of conduct to
be followed for his own good and for the good of France.

In another letter, he was to write: 'Sire, I have been
buried alive five times and am familiar with misfortune. In
order to have a more compassionate heart than the average
man, one must have suffered great hardship . . . I had the
sweet satisfaction, at the time of the Terror, to have saved
the lives of twenty-two unfortunate people . . . Petitioning
Fouquet d'Étinville (*sic*) on behalf of royalists was tantamount to my persuading him that I was one too. If I braved
death to save the lives of twenty-two citizens, judge, great
Emperor, if my heart can do other than be interested in
you, who are the saviour of my dear country.'

But all these letters remained unanswered. In his apartment
at 53 Rue des Saint-Pères, Latude no longer saw anything
coming in. The Legros were dead and his advanced age
inevitably isolated him. What was more, for several years
his fixed ideas had discouraged the few people who were
still concerned with him. Thus, a few years earlier, when
Mme Legros was still alive, the Duchesse d'Abrantès had
issued an invitation to Latude. 'When he arrived,' she wrote

in her Memoirs, 'I was truly respectful and tender, to an edifying degree, towards him. I took his hand, I led him to an armchair, I placed a pillow under his feet; in other words, had he been my grandfather I wouldn't have treated him better. At the table, I seated him on my right. But', the Duchess added, 'my enchantment was shortlived. All he could talk about were his adventures with a frightful, unbelievable loquacity.'

One friend only remained, the Chevalier de Pougens, who after having helped Latude so often, now financially secure, contributed still to the future of the Legros children. This excellent man had always given proof of infinite patience towards Latude. Did Latude send him a puzzling note requesting his assistance for a third party? The Chevalier de Pougens would immediately promise to do so, and also continued to lend small sums, or again opened his home every time Latude invited himself without warning.

It had to be admitted that, true scrounger that he was, Latude was able to bring to it his irresistible good nature. On 25 June 1804, for example, he wrote to the Chevalier de Pougens: 'Now I am warning you loud and clear that if, ten days from today, 11 Messidor, you are not in Paris, with all your cattle (the Chevalier de Pougens was at his estates at the time), I will leave the next day, that I'll arrive as hungry as a horse and as thirsty as a coachman, and when I've eaten up all your provisions and drunk your entire wine cellar down to the last bottle, I'll play the second act of the comedy of Jocriste: you'll see the plates, dishes, pots and bottles – empty of course – fly and all the furniture thrown out of the window!'

And Latude had in fact, at the age of nearly eighty, retained a lively, playful nature and was still able to enjoy the charms of existence and even with a kind of frenzy, as if he had wanted to make up for all his best years lost. Every day, he took long walks in Paris without experiencing the slightest fatigue. Those who still recognized him were surprised not to find in him a single trace of the long years of suffering endured in the royal prisons.

His only fear was the gout. And one day he felt extreme pain in his toe. Wanting to ward off the first signs of the illness, he walked the whole day long. But in the evening the pain grew to such a pitch that he had to take off his shoe, to discover a large pin stuck in his toe. With some difficulty he removed it, exclaiming: 'Thank God, it was not gout!'

Instead of gout, Latude came down with a chill during a stroll three days after Christmas in 1804. He took to his bed, persuaded that it was only a minor infection. But at his age any little problem, medically speaking, was important. He contracted pneumonia and died suddenly on 1 January 1805, when he was not quite eighty years old.

Latude did not see death coming, which was fortunate, because he dreaded it. After all, his life, interrupted for thirty-five years, had not really begun until the age when so many others were ending theirs.

A short paragraph appeared three days after his death in *Le Journal de Paris*, bearing witness to his having fallen into oblivion: 'M. Latude, famous for a thirty-five-year imprisonment in the castles of Vincennes, the Bastille and Bicêtre, died last Tuesday at the age of eighty . . . The heirs of Mme de Pompadour had made amends to him for the consequences of an act of vengeance too long drawn out and hardly in proportion to the offence . . .'

LIST OF IMPORTANT DATES

1725	*26 March*	Birth of 'Jean-Henri, illegitimate, son of Jeanneton Aubrespy and an unknown father . . .'
1748	*October*	Treaty of Aix-la-Chapelle puts an end to Jean Danry's job as assistant surgeon in the army
1749	*29 April*	Booby-trap parcel sent to Versailles
	1 May	*Lettre de cachet* imprisoning Danry in the Bastille
	end of July	Transferred to the Castle-keep of Vincennes
1750	*25 June*	Escape from Vincennes
	1 July	Danry caught and thrown into solitary confinement in Bastille dungeon
1751	*30 December*	Danry is placed in a room with a servant
1752	*spring*	Allègre shares Danry's cell
1756	*evening of 25–6 February*	Escape from the Bastille
	15 June	Danry caught and put back into the Bastille dungeon
1759	*September*	Danry transferred to a room shortly after Sartine's nomination to position of lieutenant-general of Paris police
1764	*15 April*	Death of the Marquise de Pompadour
	8 July	Allègre transferred as madman to Charenton

	16 September	Transfer of Danry, now an intolerable prisoner, from the Bastille to Vincennes
1765	*23 November*	Third escape abetted by fog
	17 December	Danry again caught and sent back to Vincennes
1774	*10 May*	Death of Louis XV
	August	Le Noir replaces Sartine
1775	*27 September*	Transfer to Charenton (where Danry henceforth goes by the name of Latude)
1777	*5 June*	Release from Charenton
	15 July	New arrest and imprisonment in Bicêtre
1781 –1782	*winter*	Beginning of Mme Legros's action on behalf of Latude
1784	*23 March*	*Lettre de cachet* ordering the final release of Latude (after thirty-five years of imprisonment)
1789	*15 July*	The day after the fall of the Bastille, Latude goes to visit the citadel; everywhere he is acclaimed as an exemplary victim of royal despotism
	autumn–winter	Publication of his first writings
1790	*spring*	First edition of the *Memoirs of Latude*, who is received at the National Assembly
1792	*25 February*	A 3,000-*livre*s pension is granted
1793	*11 September*	Lawsuit against Mme de Pompadour's heirs
1799		Two works on contemporary issues to revive 'public credit' and 'to save the Republic in less than three months'
1805	*1 January*	Death of Latude from an attack of pneumonia

APPENDIXES

I

COPY OF THE SIXTY-FIFTH LETTER
SENT TO M. DE SARTINE

From the Bastille,
10 May 1762

SIR,

I patiently bear the loss of the best years of my life and my fortune: I bear my rheumatism, the weakness in my arms and an iron band round my body for the rest of my life; but I cannot bear the loss of my cherished eyesight, it is diminishing every day. I beg you, for the love of God, to have the kindness to grant me two hours of fresh air each day in the garden, or on the towers, to help me keep the little that remains. Sir, if I have written you strongly worded letters, my eyes are the reason for it, they make me lose my mind, I'm no longer able to control myself; in short, I'm sorry and beg you pardon a thousand times over, what more could you want! either take my life once and for all or grant me the remedies that have never been refused a human being. Sir, from time immemorial all great men have been subject to disgrace. I need not mention Demosthenes, Hannibal or Cicero: all those men governed in part their states; but I will speak to you of France. You have seen Cardinal de Retz at the Bastille, at the tower of Nantes; M. le Blanc also at the Bastille, at the tower of Vincennes: you have seen the Chancellor d'Agueffeau, several times exiled to Frènes; you see the Comte de

Maurepas still today. If you were to encounter such misfortune, Sir, would you want me to be the only one to tarnish your virtues, to say that you treated me inhumanely, that you refused me remedies that animals are never denied; for what is the subject of my strongly worded letters? I don't accuse you at all for the length of my misery, but I am angry that you refuse me a two-hour walk every day in the garden or on the towers, which you grant other prisoners: when you say to me: 'What rights have you to justify demanding such a favour from me?' Alas! what rights do I have! I will not prove to you point by point the injustice done to me, for I see very well that it grieves you, but I am losing my sight; my second claim is that I'm in the fourteenth year of suffering, a frighteningly long period; my third claim, after my first escape from the tower of Vincennes, I generously turned myself in, like a lamb, into the paternal hands of the King.

It's a claim that should certainly inspire compassion for me in you; for it is not honest to abuse one's good faith cruelly. Sir, people forget a thousand acts of justice to blame an inhuman trait; you have great proof of this in the person of M. le Naigre: I believe that this judge handed out over 500 fair rulings; that he pardoned over 200 prisoners, I don't listen to people, but reasonable individuals say that this judge was surprised by a false declaration from The Man; so you see that a single inhuman characteristic has led to this judge's loss of reputation, has ruined his fortune; he's in Holland and is ashamed to say his own name. Sir, much goes into earning a good reputation; but it takes little to lose it: I therefore would not like to be the only one to complain about you; I, who at first sight based all my hopes, my happiness on that air of kindness that nature and the graces have spread over your face, I humbly ask you for a remedy, a reasonable relaxation of my regime, since you grant it today to other prisoners. I beg you, Sir, my father, with fourteen years of suffering which surely make my prayer respectable, to have the goodness to grant me this favour and in recognition, I will pray God all my life to bestow in ever greater bounty his holy blessing on you and on your entire dear family.

Yours most honourably, ac. *Signed*, DANRY

II

'DESPOTISM UNVEILED, OR THE MEMOIRS OF HENRI MASERS DE LATUDE DETAINED FOR THIRTY-FIVE YEARS IN VARIOUS STATE PRISONS . . .'

(Paris, 1792) (extract)

Soiled for so many centuries by the feebleness of its kings and the insolent despotism of their ministers, France has just finally shaken off the fetters whose weight for so long held her in bondage and of which it was believed she had the servility to be ashamed no longer. Her first glances, her first efforts, as she rose out of this shameful stupor, were directed towards the state prisons. A watchful Europe followed France's moves and applauded the courage with which she filled in those horrible abysses that concealed the moving forces of despotism, its crimes and acts of vengeance. We bless all the days, for ever happy, when we saw those shameful walls come crumbling down at the first shout of liberty. But, to have a better taste of the reward of this beneficial act, Frenchmen should know from what acts of horror they have been saved by this deed of heroism; they should learn of the infamies of which *the gods from this Tartarus* were capable and to what excessive audacity they were taken by the habit of committing them. Victim for thirty-five years of their cruelties and their hatred, I found out only too well what those atrocious truths were.

Yes, for thirty-five years I vainly wore down those infernal vaults with my sighs and my despair: my soul shattered every instant by fits of rage and continually

battered by pain; all my limbs bruised, racked by the weight
and grating of my chains; my body gnawed by the most
repellent animals; all I breathed in was putrid exhalations
instead of air; and most horrible of all, saved and given
respite each time death seemed to want to put an end to
my agony and snatch me from my executioners: that was
my fate throughout this long succession of years. All of
you, who witness time going by and flying so swiftly in
the midst of pleasures and freedom, if you can imagine that
it suspends its course for the unfortunate person moaning
away in the solitude of a dungeon, consider for a moment
how this horrible period of thirty-five years must have
seemed like centuries to a man whose torments, ever new,
made worse by what his mind was to recall from the past,
continually drained him of his courage and his strength. My
sole aim is not to stir up in you cold, sterile compassion: I
dare aspire to instruct you by my misfortunes. Seeing so
many crimes unpunished every day, you will understand
how a favourite and her shameful ministers dared to take
vengeance for a slight offence.

Follow me along the painful road on which I have
travelled too long; your mind, revolted, will often consider
unbelievable the truths that I am about to unveil to you:
but I swear that I will not recount a fact that is not one; I
can supply proof for most of them, or quote witnesses: two
of my bitterest persecutors are still alive; let them dare refute
them. Today I denounce them before the people's court,
tomorrow I shall drag them before the court of law: there
I will demand an account for each of the tears they caused
me to shed and it is on those same facts that we shall be
judged.

I was born on 23 March 1725, at the Château de Craiseih,
near Montagnac in Languedoc, on an estate belonging to
the Marquis de Latude, my father, Chevalier of the royal
military order of Saint Louis, lieutenant-colonel of the

regiment of Orléans-Dragoons, since then passed away
when King's lieutenant in Sedan. My education was that of
a gentleman destined to serve his country and his king. I
will not go into detail about my early years: the real story
of my life is only that of my misfortunes. I had shown
myself to have certain aptitudes and a definite taste for
mathematics: my parents decided to cultivate them and
favoured my inclination, which led me to enter the field of
engineering. At the age of twenty-two, my father sent me
to M. Dumai, his friend, chief engineer at Berg-op-
Zoom: he welcomed me, received me in the capacity of
supernumerary and had me assume the uniform. I was ready
for action when, unfortunately for me, the peace of 1748
was concluded. My father wanted me to take advantage of
this moment of respite: he sent me to Paris to take my
courses in mathematics and to finish my education. I was
young. I had all the activity of my age, and I continually
experienced the torment it causes in those who want to play
a part and who take the restlessness of their mind for talent.
I would have paid any price for the happiness of succeeding.
But for that I had to have patrons; I wanted them powerful;
my pride sought them in the highest ranks, or rather desire
for glory; for why degrade this passion which, in a young
man, is always a noble sentiment worthy of a certain esteem?
Whatever the case, I was not a well-known person, I wanted
to be one; and to find the means, I consulted only my
imagination: this is what it suggested to me:

The Marquise de Pompadour was in power at that time.
This imperious woman paid the price of universal hatred
for the crime of having caused the King to lose the respect
and love of his people: she had just added that of having
sacrificed to her vengeance a dear minister, whom she had
punished for an ingenious joke with disgrace and exile. Her
name was only uttered with a mixture of contempt and
horror, and in every mouth was found the expression of a
feeling that filled every heart.

One day in April 1749 I was in the Tuileries: two men
sitting next to me were talking against her with the utmost

indignation. The fire that seemed to inflame them excited my mind, which, still oriented towards the goal to which all my thoughts went, believed it had found in a plan that it then began to nurture, a sure means of bringing about my advancement and ensuring my fortune. It did not appear to me sufficient to warn the Marquise de Pompadour about public opinion; I probably would not have informed her of anything she did not already know, or about which she did not suspect. I imagined giving a greater sign of my zeal and arousing her interest in my fate through recognition. After posting a letter to her address, in which I had placed a powder which could not cause any harm, I ran to Versailles, I told her what I had heard; I exaggerated the desire that the two men had shown to fight with others for the glory to deliver France from her, and I added that I had followed them to the main post office, where they had taken a parcel, which, from their talk, I had to suspect was for her, and perhaps concealed some very subtle poison.

The first move by the Marquise was to express to me her utmost sensitivity and to offer me a purse full of gold, which I refused, telling her that I dared claim a reward more worthy of her and myself, in accordance with my state and goodwill which I had told her about. Suspicious and defiant, as tyrants are, she wanted a sample of my writing; and under the pretext of taking down and keeping my address, she made me sit at her desk to give it to her. The sheer ecstasy the success of my project caused me, and my lively nature, did not allow me to see the trap; and I did not think when tracing with the same hand the characters of the two addresses that I was going to give myself away. I returned home, proud of my work, and already calculating all the degrees of my future grandeur.

The Marquise received the parcel: she tested the powder found in it on various animals: seeing that it had nothing harmful in it, and recognizing, upon seeing the two addresses, that the same hand had written them, she considered this thoughtless blunder a bloodthirsty outrage, or rather a crime; and issued the strictest orders against me.

The following 1 May, while I was given over to dreaming the most brilliant plans, a police officer called Saint-Marc, followed by some arresting officers, came to interrupt this sweet reverie. I was at the time in furnished lodgings on the Cul-de-sac du Coq. It was around eight o'clock at night. I was thrown into a carriage and taken to the Bastille.

I was led to a low-ceilinged room, called the *council chamber*, where I found all the officers of the castle awaiting me. I was searched from head to foot: they took away all my clothes: they took away everything I had on me, money, jewelry, papers: I was given despicable rags, which had undoubtedly been impregnated with the tears of a horde of other unfortunate men. This ceremony, borrowed from the Inquisition and from highwaymen, was called 'admitting a prisoner' at the Bastille. I was told to write in a register that I had just been admitted to the Bastille: then I was led to a room in the tower, called the 'Corner Tower'. Two heavy doors were shut on me, and I was left alone without being informed of my crime and unaware of my fate. The next day M. Berryer, who was then lieutenant of police, came to question me. I shall mention this worthy magistrate often, and I must describe his person. He is content, when most men's pity is tired of the tale of so many misfortunes, to be able to pause for a moment with the idea of an honest human being whose touching sensitivity has sometimes softened them: I was not able to enjoy this sad advantage very often.

M. Berryer inspired confidence by his gentleness and kindness. In order to do what was proper, he dared to place himself above biased opinion and, in the exercise of his functions, only consulted his heart and duty. He is little known today; it should not come as a surprise; there were only poor men at the time. A man like this was displaced by the Marquise's Court.

I did not conceal from him either what I had done or the goal I had set myself: my candour interested him; he only saw youthful spirits in this action, perhaps excusable because of its reason, worthy at the most, in any case, of a light correction. He promised that he would defend me before Madame de Pompadour and ask her for my freedom: but a man who dared to contradict her passion and not to take harsh revenge for his injuries enjoyed little credit in her mind. He found her inflexible and was forced to confess it to me . . .

LATUDE, OR THIRTY-FIVE YEARS OF CAPTIVITY

A historical melodrama in three acts and five scenes,
preceded by
A Morning at Trianon

Prologue by Messrs G. De Pixèrecourt and A. Bourgeois

Prologue

[In the garden of Trianon, at Versailles, a young, handsome engineering officer, Masers de Latude, asks a young milkmaid named Henriette, who is not insensitive to his charm, the shortest way to the Marquise de Pompadour's. He has fallen madly in love with this woman. There he meets a musketeer called Dalègre, who also wants to see the King's mistress. Could he also be in love with the Marquise?]

Dalègre: In love! with the King's mistress, the most handsome man in France? Oh! no, that would be too presumptuous.

Latude: You're right, I really think I've lost my head.

Dalègre: Poor fool! I should have suspected that when I saw you wearing her colours. A Pompadour sword bow! that says it all.
      (Latude has a blue bow attached to his sword)

Latude: You said it, poor fool! I'd give my blood, my life for the least of her favours.

Dalègre: It won't cost you that much.

Latude: What blasphemy!

Dalègre: The goddess deigns to become a human sometimes.
   M. de Machault and the Abbé de Bernis know something
   about that.

Latude: What do you mean, M. Dalégre! You think . . .?

Dalègre: With women, everything depends on their passing
   fancy and the moment. Those who look the most severe
   are always flattered when they inspire a wild passion; that
   only adds to the high opinion they have of themselves.
   I've come for a motive entirely different from yours.

Latude (to himself): So much the better.

Dalègre: Yesterday a group of us young fellows got together
   for supper. I sang some naughty songs about the Marquise;
   and this morning, my captain told me that I no longer
   had the honour of belonging to the musketeers. You'll
   understand that I'm not going to stand for that.

Latude: What do you intend to do?

Dalègre: To fight the King's favourite. She wants to subject
   the whole of France to her whims and acts of revenge;
   to tell her face to face all my thoughts, and to threaten
   her with the revelation of all I know, first to her royal
   lover, then to the public.

Latude: You say I'm a fool, but I think you're not very
   good yourself.

*[Police officer Saint-Marc arrives to arrest Dalègre, who is still
holding some nasty verses against the Marquise de Pompadour
which he has just read to Latude. In a burst of generosity, Latude
takes them, so as not to compromise the poor musketeer, who is
being hauled off, by order of the King, to the Bastille.
Latude had written to Mme de Pompadour warning her against a
parcel of poison being mailed to her. He had overheard a plot.
But the King's physician, Dr. Quesnay, compares the two*

*handwritings and uncovers Latude's rather crude booby trap. He
informs the Marquise who still wants to receive Latude. But the
lieutenant of police is roaming about in the vicinity . . .]*

The Marquise: I have agreed to receive you sir; your letter
was of great interest to me and I did not want to leave
you waiting for a sign of my recognition. But you were
a bit too fast in sending me this so-called poison. I know
it all and can only see in it a very damnable act of deceit
which would get you a harsh sentence if the magistrates
responsible for public order were to be informed of the
matter.

Latude: Yes, Madam, I'm out of my mind, but if you could
deign to listen to me, I shall not have invoked your
generous pity in vain.

The Marquise: Speak, sir.

(She sits down)

Latude: One of my relatives, a friend of your uncle, M. de
Tournehem, and like him a lover of the arts, often
attended your delightful parties. He took me to Étioles
five years ago. There I was fortunate enough to see you
play what was the perfect role for you, in which the
author had given you the means to take advantage of
your talents which you possess in such rare perfection!
. . . Recently arrived from my province and devoted
entirely to serious studies, I had only encountered a few
occasions for exercise of my judgement on the arts in
which you excel . . .

The Marquise: Sir, you're flattering too much.

Latude: No, Madam, I'm not exaggerating at all. That
delightful and fatal evening brought about a drastic change
in me. For the past five years, my only thought, my sole
desire has been to see you and hear you speak . . . I
looked for you everywhere, but adverse fate each time
led you away from me. Finally, the day before yesterday,
a ray of hope came to revive my heart. I was sitting in

the Tuileries gardens under the majestic chestnut trees, two men whose faces were hidden in the shadow were also sitting by the same tree. They spoke of you in rather harsh terms.

The Marquise: Well sir! What did they say?

Latude: They blamed the weakness of the King and that of his rather cowardly ministers, as they said, for succumbing to a woman. Their deathly desires went so far as to wish for your death, which would be the liberation of France. I walked away from those wretched men, they disgusted me; but I discovered in their dreadful talk a means of seeing you and proceeded to carry through with it. If it is a crime, it began with a passion which always finds an excuse in a woman's heart. It's so sweet to feel love as I feel it! Being in love is to devote your entire self to the person of your choice in such a way that you only live, think and act according to that person and for that person; it is to feel capable of the noblest actions, of the most generous devotion, of every sacrifice to equal the beloved object, to prove your tenderness, to ensure that person's happiness; it means feeling for another creature everything I've felt for you these past five years.

(He throws himself at the feet of the Marquise, takes her hand and smothers it in passionate kisses)

Scene xviii

Lieutenant of Police, Latude, Marquise, Henriette, Footman

Lieutenant of Police (coming out of the pavilion): Poor wretch! such audacity will be punished. You'll perish at the Bastille.

Marquise: He's a fool!

Lieutenant of Police: He's insulted the King, he's overheard
   State secrets, he'll have plenty of time to forget all that
   in the dungeon. Get him searched!
         (The footman approaches, Latude moves back and
            empties everything out of his pockets. Dalègre's
                                    writings are found)

The Marquise (to herself): Poor young man!
            (The lieutenant of police reads the lines and
                                    seems disgusted)

Lieutenant of Police: You're sorry for him, Madam? Look at
   whom you pity.

Latude (to himself): Dalègre's rhymes! I won't betray him.

*Marquise (after reading and returning the tablets to the Lieutenant
   of Police):* Oh . . . Do your duty, Sir.

Henriette (to herself): Poor man! I'm the cause of his downfall!
            (Latude is taken away, continuing to look at
               the Marquise tenderly, given up to his
               delirious passion. Henriette weeps)

                           Act I

*[Henriette Legros, the young milkmaid who had met Latude in
the Trianon gardens, has left Versailles to live in Paris. She has
a room overlooking the Bastille where poor Latude has been
imprisoned. It goes without saying that she has fallen in love with
him as she tells a good neighbour, Mother Marguerite:]*

Mother Marguerite: Poor girl, what a touching story. I'm
   deeply moved; but tell me, you knew how to read and
   write then!

Henriette: No, I learned for him.

Mother Marguerite: And embroidery?

Henriette: Also for him.

Mother Marguerite: Good little angel! All this amazing work! Wouldn't two diligent workers have difficulty in accomplishing all this?

Henriette (almost ashamed as she stares at the ground): It's also for him.

Mother Marguerite: And those beautiful eyes which I've often seen red and swollen in the morning after a long sleepless night . . . and the result of this embroidery for which I hear so much praise and which you ask me to turn almost all into gold, because you spend hardly a sixth of what you earn on yourself, is it also the little messenger (*pointing to the pigeon*) that takes it to him?

Henriette (even more embarrassed): Yes, Mother Marguerite. The prisoners' food is so bad! Their treatment so cruel! The cold so freezing! So isn't it my duty to ease the suffering I've caused . . . All I ask from heaven is to live as long as his captivity lasts.

Mother Marguerite (touched, wiping away the tears): Heaven owes you more than that, my child. It will reward you for so much hardship endured; I'm telling you, and I draw this conviction out of my heart. No, this charitable, pious work will not remain unrewarded. Another question, because now you can no longer hide anything from me. How did you get that pigeon?

Henriette: By chance. I was sitting in front of this window, and as long as there's daylight, my eyes never leave my work, except to glance at the tower where the only one who gives me reason to live is languishing. One evening, I saw a white pigeon struggling at the narrow opening where the light reaches as far as my poor friend . . . it returned the next day, the days after that, and the idea dawned on me of using the bird to communicate with my prisoner. I placed this board on the windowsill and put some bread crumbs on it. Fluttering about, the pigeon discovered my little store and ate greedily; it then let me caress it; finally, I dared to attach a paper under its wing. The prisoner guessed my idea and when the bird came back I found a reply. How happy did I feel? I'm sure you can imagine. Henri was going to read my heart, I was going to read his. From that moment on, a new existence was to begin for both of us.

Mother Marguerite: What a lovely story! my dear sweet little neighbour . . . I can't tell you how much you interest me and how much I love you! . . . (*She kisses her hands, joyfully*) And I didn't know any of this; for the past fifteen to eighteen months, I was surprised to see you were eating more; I was glad, I was delighted. Now I would say to myself, my little neighbour has a good appetite; so much the better, that proves her health is better, and I'm overjoyed. I truly scarcely suspected that there was ordinary fare here . . . Dear child! A thousand thanks for the pleasure you have given me!

[Henriette is fortunate enough to see the prisoner each day when he goes for a walk on the platform of the formidable fortress. She communicates with him through the pigeons flying between her window and the loophole of the dungeon cell. Latude's messages are written in his own blood]

[The second scene is that of a room at the Bastille. Seven years have passed since Latude's imprisonment. But he has been preparing his escape for months]

Scene i

Latude alone

(When the curtain goes up, the left-hand corner is lighted by a candle, the right-hand is in the dark. Latude is in a hole up to his waist in the middle of the room where he has taken two boards

up. He finishes measuring his ladder with his arm which is equal to one ell.)

A hundred and eighty feet! . . . according to my calculations, that's the correct length from the platform down to the moat. *(He puts his ladder back into the hole, gets out and sits on the edge.)* This has been a long and tiring stint. I took out and measured my entire ladder; I've made sure nothing is missing. Thank heaven and thanks to my tireless perseverance, it's all over. I'll wait until the first foggy night to escape. There are many such in the month of February. If I succeed in escaping, I'll certainly have accomplished the most daring and incredible feat ever conceived by man. Without anyone's help, to obtain these huge amounts of material, to hide it from all eyes, to work for 580 nights without waking my many watchdogs, to chain up, so to say, all their senses, to prevent them from seeing, hearing, or even suspecting, to foresee and overcome a thousand obstacles which every day and every minute should have multiplied and thwarted the execution of my plan! If I fail, no one will ever believe the boldness of this undertaking; but if I succeed . . . what a surprise for France! what glory for me! what joy for my dear Henriette! . . . Oh! I hope. Minds of genius create, and I have one that comes from despair *(a knocking sound is heard from below, Latude was about to put the floor boards back; stops).* Am I mistaken? There is repeated knocking against the ceiling below . . . if it's a trap . . . I mustn't reply. *(The knocking is heard again.)* My God! Would the noise I made this past night have alerted my guards . . . if my secret were discovered! . . . if such misfortune were to befall me, I'd remain without courage or strength . . . my only salvation would be death . . . *(He goes back into the hole.)* Let's listen a bit closer . . . *(He bends down.)* I have the impression someone is working on the ceiling . . . perhaps it's a fellow sufferer . . . if I knew! I'd go to meet him! My efforts would be equal to his. A stone is moving!

[It is Dalègre, the musketeer arrested the same day as Latude. They meet again. The two young men decide to continue to prepare their escape together, at the price of countless difficulties. Did the cruel Saint-Marc ('ironic role', the production indicates,

'he jokes while clapping a prisoner in irons') have some premonition and decide at the last minute to have Latude removed from his room and locked up for good in the dungeon?]

Scene x

Latude alone

Cowards! . . . kill me . . . pierce a stiletto through my heart, but don't let me die a long agonizing death. Yes! yes! tonight will be the last of my captivity or the last of my life . . . Tomorrow, at the break of day, I'll be far from here, or my body will be lying at the foot of this wall. (*Flurries of snow blow in through the loophole and fall inside the prison.*) The weather is on my side . . . visibility will be poor tonight . . . Come on! . . . Help . . . Dalègre. (He knocks twice in the fireplace hearth, then he listens and soon hears Dalègre's reply.) To work! . . . the executioners won't be here till tomorrow.

[Finally, Latude and Dalègre escape after crossing the Bastille ramparts and moat]

Act II

[Latude and Dalègre have left for Amsterdam where Henriette has gone to join them. But police officer Saint-Marc also arrives in Amsterdam disguised as a merchant. Despite several cunning moves by Dalègre to save his friend, the implacable policeman ends up arresting both of them and drags them back to the Bastille. Overcome by despair, the unfortunate Henriette tries to put an end to her life, but is saved at the last minute].

Act III

[We are in a courtyard at the prison of Bicêtre. Twenty-seven more years have passed. La Pompadour is no longer alive, but the hatred of the ministers and the police has once again clapped the irons on poor Latude, now become unrecognizable. He is bald, his face wasted away and unrecognizable, covered with a long white beard. He walks like a man exhausted with age. Dalègre,

more fortunate, has gone mad, believing himself to be a police officer and wanting to arrest everyone. But the hour of justice has finally struck. Henriette Legros, who had appealed in vain to the King, Queen and ministers, has succeeded in coming in contact with Malesherbes, whose name alone evokes happiness and virtue:]

Malesherbes: (To the prisoners) Men, the King himself has sent me to you. I am charged with a mission worthy of the prince who entrusted it with me, worthy of myself who have accepted it with joy. I have come to put an end to too long a period of ill fortune. Is there someone here who goes by the name of Latude? *(Silence)* Don't let yourselves be intimidated by possible threats made against you. If M. de Latude is among you, would he please step forward and say his name. I have come to free him. The hatred of his enemies can no longer harm him.

(Silence prevails)

Lenoir: Well sir, do you still have your doubts? I told you that this man wasn't here.

Malesherbes (painfully): Oh, Sir, what have you done with him then?

(Noise off-stage. Henriette comes running on
in the utmost disorder)

Scene xv

*Saint-Marc, Lenoir, Henriette, Malesherbes, Saint-Luc, Guards,
Prisoners*

Henriette: M. de Malesherbes, you are being deceived.

Lenoir: That woman is here again!

Malesherbes: What do you say?

Henriette: He's lying! The prisoners are not all here. Two are missing.

Lenoir (in a loud voice): Who told you that?

Henriette: Oh! it's true! Just look at how pale you are! (*To M. de Malesherbes*) A short time ago a poor madman and old friend of Latude, whose name is Dalègre, came to me as if a stroke of reason had guided him. He called me by my name and dragged me rather than took me to the door of an underground cell. 'There's still one more,' he said to me, 'I'm sure of it, I'm the one who arrested him.' Then he disappeared. Oh, Sir, order this prisoner to be brought before you. Don't let his gaolers have the time to become his executioners.

Malesherbes: You tricked me sir
   Who is this man?

Saint-Marc: A dangerous lunatic named Jédor who has nothing to do with . . .

Malesherbes: Have him brought here this instant!

Saint-Marc (hesitantly): But . . .

Malesherbes (with authority): Are you forgetting that I speak in the King's name? Have you forgotten that there is justice in France?

Saint-Marc (to himself): Oh well! since I have to.

Lenoir: I didn't want to object to your having the man brought here. You'll see him, sir; but I can only remind you that he's mad and dangerous at that. He's out of his mind and is capable of anything. Public safety required that . . . There he is!

Scene xviii

Saint-Marc, Lenoir, Latude, Henriette, Malesherbes, Saint-Luc, Guards, Prisoners.

Henriette (running towards Latude): At last! . . . (*Stopping all of a sudden, and turning towards Malesherbes after closely examining the prisoner*) Oh my God, it's not him!

Latude (in a weak voice): Where are you taking me? Am I going to meet death at last? I thank you for it.

Malesherbes: By God, look at the state he's in!

Saint-Luc and the Prisoners: It's father Jédor!

Lenoir (to Malesherbes): You see, they recognize him.

Malesherbes (to Latude): Come closer, my friend.

Latude: Who are you, sir? Oh! I've been exposed to every torture, every torment; let me die in peace.

Lenoir: Did you hear him? Saint-Marc.

Malesherbes: One moment, is it true that your name is Jédor?

Latude: Me!

Malesherbes: Oh! don't be afraid of answering.

Latude: You see sir, it is not fear but despair that shuts my mouth . . . You're not the only one I've told my name and misfortunes to. They felt sorry for me, but the next day, I was put in shackles again; I was punished for having inspired pity . . . if I speak (*With joy*) Oh! if I speak, they'll kill me, maybe . . . but at least I'll no longer return to that horrible cell . . . yes, to you sir; I'll say my name to all of you; I'm neither Danry nor Jédor. I'm Latude; and these are my executioners.

Henriette (throwing her arms around Latude): Oh! I knew he was here. Latude . . . my friend . . . you're saved . . . oh my God! my God! I shall go mad with it.

Latude (in a daze): But it's impossible! Henriette! . . .

Henriette: Yes, Henriette! dear Latude, M. de Malesherbes is granting you freedom.

Latude: M. de Malesherbes! . . . he's a God to me. (*He falls to his knees in front of M. de Malesherbes*) Henriette, M. de Malesherbes, freedom! Oh, my God! . . . don't let me die now . . .
> (He falls almost in a faint; he is surrounded, Henriette kneels before him)

Henriette: My friend! . . .

Malesherbes (to Lenoir): Sir, here is the order to release M. de Latude immediately. Later, you'll have to account for all he has suffered.

Lenoir: To whom then?

Malesherbes: To the King to begin with and then to posterity which will no longer separate the name of the persecutors from that of the victim.

Dalègre (running in the background and seizing Lenoir by the collar): In the name of the King! I arrest you! . . .
> (The curtain drops to the applause of all the prisoners)

THE END

The play was presented for the first time at the *théâtre de la Gaïté* in Paris on 15 November 1834. It was staged four years after the famous three days of insurrection known to Frenchmen as Les Trois Glorieuses and the proclamation of the July monarchy. It was a time when the Romantics were evolving the ideas of social progress and political involvement. Within this context, it is easier to understand why this melodrama, which took liberties with history and which contained a multitude of romantic clichés, received such a favourable welcome from liberal critics.

The play rapidly grew to be an enormous popular success. 'Latude continues to play to a packed house', a journalist wrote in the issue of December 1834 of *La Revue du théâtre*. Fifteen days later, the same review reported: 'Latude has beaten the records of success and outranked *The Wandering Jew*, of colossal memory.' And again a fortnight later: 'Latude is a gold mine. At six o'clock each evening, there isn't a single seat left for sale.'

The play was put on throughout the reign of Louis-Philippe and under the Second Empire. During the entr'acte, the theatre hall was transformed into a museum where Vestier's portrait painting of Latude was displayed, together with the rope ladder and home-made tools used to escape from the Bastille; two enormous keys from the Bastille with a small-scale model of it sculptured from one of the stones taken from the demolition; and an autographed letter from Latude addressed to the Marquise de Pompadour.

These different objects were first displayed in 1789 at the Town Hall, then in a room at the Louvre, before becoming the property of a former lieutenant-colonel of civil engineering, a fanatical collector of objects dating back to the Revolution, of which he was able finally to form a small museum.

Meanwhile the written version of *Latude, or Thirty-five Years of Captivity* became a best-seller and went into twenty successive editions. Latude, fallen into oblivion after being in vogue during the initial years of the Revolution, was revived as History.

IV

LATUDE, HERO OF A SERIAL

The 1888 edition [Paris, Fayard, m.d.] of *Memoirs of Latude Written by Himself after the 1792 Edition* is as whimsical as the story told in Pixérécourt's play. The romanticized and popular 625-page illustrated quarto version highlights the story *per se* with many swashbuckling episodes and sentimental adventures in the taste of the serialized novel which was all the rage at the time.

The following is an excerpt from an episode in which the evil lieutenant of police, who is out to get Danry, tries to use the most infamous means to dissuade the beautiful, kind, devoted Mme Legros from helping the prisoner at Bicêtre. Mme Legros has just been summoned to the lieutenant of police (Latude is the narrator of the story):

The summons came as quite an event to the humble, peaceful household of my dear liberator.

M. Legros was dismayed by it, his wife saddened and alarmed. If lightning had struck at their feet, it would not have had a more terrible effect. After a moment of silence, the husband said with much effort:

'You must notify the Cardinal and M. Duchesne in case something should happen to you.'

'Well, what do you expect they're going to do to me?'

'Arrest you,' Legros replied, trying to hold back the tears.

'They wouldn't dare!' the courageous young woman stated. 'In any case, it's ten o'clock in the morning and I have to be at Châtelet at three o'clock. Neither of us has the time to run over to Versailles. But, if I'm not back by five this evening, take a cab and go to the Cardinal's with a letter that you can leave there if he isn't at home.'

'My God!' Legros groaned, 'What a terrible thought!'

'There's no need to be afraid,' his wife continued. 'And not a single word about this to our parents, whatever happens. Absolute silence. My mother would be screaming aloud and end up foiling our plans. As for what to do, consult M. de la Croix. I've already given him some notes for a memorandum and he knows all about the matter.'

Several hours went by in this almost funereal atmosphere. M. Legros had never understood better than at that moment the full horror of 'at his Majesty's pleasure'.

Imagining his wife on the verge of being thrown into some horrible prison like the Madelonnettes without trial, he said to himself: 'Yes! This Latude must be freed! . . . The Bastille must fall!'

Instead of regretting at this terrible moment that his wife had sacrificed herself for a sacred cause, he admired her even more and swore that he would serve the cause with renewed ardour.

But what a heartrending moment when the couple, so tenderly united in heart and mind, had to say farewell! . . .

'When I approached the cradle where our child was sleeping,' Mme Legros told me, 'I felt my strength fail; when I kissed that dear little one whom I feared I would never see again, I wet his face with tears and walked away sobbing. I was in such a state that I didn't dare to go to say goodbye to my mother. She was ill . . . Would I see her again? I asked myself. Finally, I rinsed my eyes in cold water. My husband went to fetch a cab for me and I jumped in to conceal my grief from the curiosity of the neighbours.'

Mr. Lenoir was waiting for her. She was immediately summoned before him as soon as she arrived.

I leave it to my benefactress to continue with the story.

'When I arrived at Châtelet, I had recovered my calm

and, prepared for the worst, I felt no fear. I was not made to wait. I was summoned immediately.

'The lieutenant of police, seated at a table covered with papers, which he seemed to be reading, perhaps to put on a good face, motioned me to a chair facing him and said to me:

'"Sit down."

'I waited for him to question me. He resumed in a brief tone and looked at me surreptitiously.

'"You are Mme Legros, a haberdasher who lives on the Rue des Fossés-Saint-Germain-l'Auxerrois?"

'"Yes, sir."

'"You'd do better taking care of your household and your little shop instead of getting yourself mixed up in something that's none of your business – You're in contact with a prisoner at Bicêtre named Jédor, who calls himself the Marquise de Latude, are you not?"

'I remained silent.

'"Well, speak up! Say something! . . ." the magistrate said with brutal impatience.

'I overcame my indignation and replied:

'"I know M. Mazers de Latude, imprisoned at Bicêtre under the name of Jédor. I learned of his existence and misfortunes from a manuscript, a memorandum that he had addressed to President de Gourgues, which I found lying in the street."

'This calm, measured language gave him food for thought. He stared at me attentively and said:

'"You're a cunning gossip."

'I was too small a haberdasher to reply to such an impertinent remark.

'"You're a schemer," he added.

'I let him continue talking and did not say a word.

'"I'd like to know, I shall know, what motivates you to want to help get this madman released from Bicêtre. To obtain confessions which I don't expect you'll give of your own accord, I have irresistible means, and that you know very well. And to obtain a pardon, which you'll need after the criminal activities you're embroiled in, you have to confess the whole truth to me. Well, Legros, tell us whose interest, or whom you are serving by intervening on behalf of the insane Jédor who calls himself Latude?".

"'Sir, I serve only a feeling of pity and charity."

"'Don't go telling me such nonsense. We're used to penetrating the darkest consciences. I'll ask you again. For the second time, I invite you to tell the truth."

"'I am telling the truth, and if you're thinking of torturing me, you won't get any other reply."

"'Wasn't it an agent of the Duc d'Orléans who contacted you?"

"I don't know of anyone."

"I know someone is behind you, encouraging you."

"I don't require advice or encouragement from anyone."

"But you need money?"

'I turned purple with shame at the insinuation.

"'You're being paid secretly, ha! You look worried . . . I put my finger on it."

"'Oh! how abominable!" I cried with indignation.

"'Let's have no play-acting here now!" said M. Lenoir. 'You're not dealing here with a townsman from the Rue des Fossés-Saint-Germain. I know that you're in financial straits. Your business is not doing well; your husband earns little. You have a child. You're supporting your parents. Your father well along in his years and your mother infirm, and your means are insufficient. How do you pay for everything and still find enough money to buy presents for your protégé and to pay expenses for your clothes and transport, which you need to do all this? I have mathematical proof here that your alleged resources are not enough."

"'But, Sir . . .'"

"'Don't deny it! . . . I know too that you don't have any debts, because you have no credit. So you're getting help from somewhere? Some gifts? . . .'"

"'Sir, I swear to you!"

"'Don't wait for me to tell you who opens his purse for you; speak up."

"'No, Sir, I'm waiting for you to tell me. I'm curious to know what slander is behind the accusations you're casting at me."

"'I repeat my question: Have you been receiving outside help?"

"'No, sir."

"'Presents, if you prefer; but presents suggest a lover. Will you let your moral purity come under suspicion in order to explain your means of existence?"

"'Oh! that's going too far!" I cried, covering my face with my hands.

"'No sentimentality, my dear lady. A magistrate must have a certain harshness in his language, and like a surgeon, he doesn't operate without pain. Why do you force me to these hurtful suppositions by your denials? Besides, I'm only repeating what everyone says in your neighbourhood. They claim that M. de Rohan is supporting you . . . These are the words of base, ignorant people. The mistress of a prince, even if she is only a passing pleasure, doesn't stay in such a lowly position. In my opinion, you're being supported with a little money and egged on by a lot of promises from an agent working for the Duc d'Orléans.

'And as I raised my head and seemed relieved of a great burden:

"'Ah! there we are!" said M. Lenoir.

'Not at all, sir," I cried.

'The lieutenant of police then appeared to be at the end of his patience and thought for a moment.

"'The matter has to be cleared up, he said; whether you're hiding something or not, I see you're not going to shed any light on the case of your own accord. My policemen will have to obtain the information for me. But I want to nip any public agitation in the bud before it gets started. However indifferent you may be to that, it is a troublesome matter for us. Latude's dossier has been sent to the King. I hear that you respect the King's judgement and therefore don't want you to petition anyone for what only His Majesty can grant. So you will stop being a nuisance, Madam, with your requests. You will also cease from your assiduous attentions at the Rohan household. In a word, you're going to promise me that you won't do anything more in favour of the man whose cause you've espoused."

"'I can't make a promise I won't keep, sir."

"'I'll have you locked up."

"'I've been expecting that for a long time," I said.

"'And do you think you'll become a martyr?" said M. Lenoir ironically.

'"I've not done anything rashly, and from the very start I knew what I was exposing myself to.

'"And what will become of those who through blood and the moral law should be most dear to you, your sick mother, your baby in the cradle, your husband?

'"I have my husband's consent," I replied, a little shaken by a question that evoked the most touching memories for me.

'" Before coming here, my husband and I talked about what we would have to do, if you should use your arbitrary power to keep me in prison. Have me locked up, Monsieur Lieutenant of Police; you'll then have to have my husband imprisoned, his grief will be a scandal to you. Don't stop there. Throw our child into a home. That'll be what you call hushing up an affair. You'll see what the public thinks of it."

'"The public! . . . Your reasoning is of the falsest and most impertinent nature!" M. Lenoir shouted. Your mind is set with horrible prejudices and you think that the government lives by arbitrary power. Rid yourself of such illusions.

We live under a prince who is the enemy of fraud.

You'll remain free . . ."

'I could not restrain a start of surprise.

'"Yes," the lieutenant of police continued," you can go now . . . But don't forget, I shall have my eye on you. Day by day, hour by hour, I shall be kept informed of your every move, and if you continue to place us in an embarrassing situation and to corrupt public opinion, I'll send you to the Madelonnettes in the interests of public order. – I've spoken. Go, Madam, and mend your ways."

'I stood up, said goodbye and left.'

Bibliography

MANUSCRIPT SOURCES

Bibliothèque de l'Arsenal (Bastille Archives)

Mainly MSS 11692 and 11693

Miscellaneous: MSS 11925, 11926, 11931, 11943, 12165, 12727

Correspondence between the Paris lieutenant-general of police and the governor or major of the Bastille: MSS 12499, 12500, 12502, 12503, 12504, 12505, 12506, 12519

NB In bundles 11692 and 11693, dealing entirely with the Latude case, there is, as a matter of curiosity, the envelope of the booby-trap parcel and pieces of cloth written with the prisoner's blood.

Archives de la Préfecture de Police

Bastille Archives, boxes Bastille I (a few references); Bastille IV (fos. 612, 614ff., 860ff.)

Musée Carnavalet (Reserve)

E. 105^{37} 1D20

NB Also in the museum are Latude's portrait painted in 1789 by Antoine Vestier, the rope ladder used to escape from the Bastille in 1756 and, in the Reserve, Latude's flute which is used as a clasp for a copy of the Memoirs, the bequest of M. Théodore Lorin, secretary to M. de Pougens.

Archives nationales

Minutes of the commissioners from Châtelet Y 15811 A, B; Y12216
Petition by Latude to the Revolutionary Assemblies and the Executive Directory. ₑ 7.7216

Bibliothèque nationale (Department of Manuscripts)

FF nouv. acq. 308, 3241, 11365, 22220

Bibliothèque historique de la Ville de Paris

MSS 479, MS 717 (res 19), 776 (fo. 63ff.)

Musée de l'Histoire vivante, Ville de Montreuil

Letter, undated

Registre de l'état civil de Montagnac, arr. de Béziers, dépt. de l'Hérault

26 March 1725

Bibliothèque municipale de Rouen

Leber Fund MSS 5326, 5822, 5831

PRINTED SOURCES

Many of Latude's letters published or analysed in various sales catalogues of autographs.

Other letters published in various reviews (mainly *Revue rétrospective* and *Nouvelle revue rétrospective*) and in various works: e.g. Delort, M. J., *Histoire de la détention des philosophes et des gens de lettres à la Bastille et à Vincennes* (History of the detention of philosophers and men of letters at the Bastille and Vincennes), vol. 3 (Paris, 1824)

Histoire d'une détention de trente-neuf ans dans les prisons d'État,
écrite par le prisonnier lui-même (1787). (History of thirty-
nine years of detention in State prisons, written by the
prisoner himself).

Le Donjon de Vincennes, la Bastille et Bicêtre, mémoire de
   M. Masers de Latude, gentilhomme languedocien, détenu dans
   les prisons d'État pendant trente-neuf ans; avec la lettre du
   Marquis de Beaupoil à M. de Bergasse sur l'histoire de M. de
   Latude et sur les ordres arbitraires (1787). (The keep of
   Vincennes, the Bastille and Bicêtre, memoir of M. Masers
   de Latude, Languedoc gentleman locked up in the State
   prisons for thirty-nine years; with the letter from the
   Marquis de Beaupoil to M. de Bergasse on the story of
   M. de Latude and on arbitrary orders)
NB These two successive editions are not by Latude (who
   denounced them as forgeries in 1790 when the first edition
   of his *Memoirs* was published), but by the Marquis
   Beaupoil de Saint-Aulaire. However, their interest lies in
   the fact that they were the only works published before
   the Revolution and were part of the many semi–clandestine
   works which proliferated in France during the reign of
   Louis XVI. Another undated edition some thirty pages
   long and of doubtful authenticity had probably been
   published in 1785, shortly after Latude's release, under
   the title, *Relation des emprisonnements et des évasions des*
   châteaux de la Bastille, de Vincennes et de Bicêtre, de Henri
   Mazers De la Tude, ingénieur, écrite par lui-même en décembre
   1782. (An account of imprisonments and escapes from
   the châteaux of the Bastille, Vincennes and Bicêtre by
   Henri Mazers De la Tude, engineer, written by himself
   in December 1782)

Mémoire de M. Delatude, ingénieur, 1789 (31 pages)
NB Here Latude tells the story of his escape from the
   Bastille during the night of 25–6 February 1756. It was
   his first work.

Mémoire adressé à Mme la Marquise de Pompadour, par
   M. Danry prisonnier à la Bastille et trouvé au greffe de cette
   prison d'État, le lendemain de sa prise par les Parisiens; suivi
   des 65, 66 et 67e lettres du même prisonnier à M. de Sartine,
   et de quatre autres à MM. Quénay et Duval (1789).

(Memoir addressed to the Marquise de Pompadour, by
M. Danry prisoner at the Bastille and found in the archives
of this State prison the day after it was captured by
Parisians; followed by the 65th, 66th and 67th letters from
the same prisoner to M. de Sartine and by four others to
Messrs. Quénay and Duval, 1789)

*Le Despotisme dévoilé, ou Mémoires de Henri Masers de Latude,
détenu pendant trente-cinq ans dans diverses prisons d'État,
rédigés sur les pièces originales par M. Thiéry . . . (1790)*
(Despotism unveiled, or Memoirs of Henri Masers de
Latude, locked up for thirty-five years in various State
prisons written from the original documents by M. Thiéry
. . . 1790)
NB This is the official version of Latude's *Memoirs*, printed
at his expense and written by the lawyer Thiéry. It was
tremendously successful and was re-edited in 1792 and in
1793. Another edition appeared in 1835 along with a re-
edition of the apocryphal *Memoirs* of 1787. (This first
renewal of interest was triggered off by the success of
the play that had then just been written and was an
entirely romanticized and romantic version of Latude's
captivity – see extracts in appendix.) Other editions of
these *Memoirs* were published in the late ninteenth and
early twentieth centuries at the celebration of the centennial
of the fall of the Bastille. These reprints, often erroneous,
are not to be confused with the entirely fictitious versions
that retained the title of *Mémoires* (see extracts in
appendixes).

*Discours de M. de Latude sur le despotisme dévoilé, prononcé à
la barre de l'Assemblée nationale, par M. Thiéry (1790)*
(Speech by M. de Latude on despotism unveiled, presented
before the National Assembly by M. Thiéry, 1790)

*Projet de coalition de 83 départmeents de la France pour sauver la
République en moins de trois mois, par Henri Mazère Latude,
an VIII*
(Proposal for a coalition of 83 French departments to save
the Republic in less than three months, by Henri Mazère
Latude, year VIII)

*Mémoire sur les moyens de rétablir le crédit public et l'ordre dans
les finances de la France, par le citoyen Latude, an VIII.*

(Pamphlet on the means of restoring public credit and putting order in France's finances, by citizen Latude, year VIII)

Mémoires authentiques de Latude, écrits par lui au donjon de Vincennes et à Charenton, publiés d'après le manuscrit de Saint-Pétersbourg . . . (Paris, n.d.) [1910]
(Authentic memoirs of Latude, written by himself in the keep of Vincennes and at Charenton, published after the manuscript of Saint Petersburg . . .)
NB This is the edition by F. Funck-Brentano of the Saint Petersburg MS, the story of Latude's detention written by himself at Vincennes and Charenton from 1756 to 1777 with the title of *Grand Mémoire ou Rêveries du sieur de M.* [Masers de la Tude] *écrites de sa main dans le donjon de Vincennes et à la Bastille de 1775 à 1778.*
Great Memoir or Musings by Sir (Masers de la Tude) written in his own hand in the keep of Vincennes and at the Bastille from 1775 to 1778). Despite its incomplete and disjointed nature and the sometimes delirious phrases, not to mention the flat style, this 150-page text is interesting in that it was written by Latude while in prison.
   Moreover, the story deserves to be told. The MS was confiscated from Latude upon his arrest in 1777, shortly after his release from Charenton. Stored at the Bastille, the document was first recovered by a collector in the moats of the Bastille where the citadel's archives lay strewn on the day after 14 July 1789. The attaché from the Russian embassy, Pierre Doubrowsky, a passionate collector, bought it along with several other MSS. This justifiably famous collection was acquired by the Russian government in 1805 and was added to the already rich collection of French MSS in the Imperial Library of St Petersburg. The Arsenal Library acquired a copy in 1886 which fortunately completed the Latude archives (Bastille Arch., end of bundle 11693). Published in part in 1886, the 'St Petersburg MS' was finally published in 1910 under the auspices of Frantz Funck-Brentano, the then curator of the Arsenal Library (*Mémoires authentiques* . . .).

FURTHER SOURCES

Biographical note by Jal in the *Dictionnaire critique de biographie et d'histoire* (Paris, 1867)

Preface and index by Georges Bertin to the 1904 edn of *Mémoires de Masers de Latude* . . . (faithful re-edition of the 1790 text)

Mémoires de la Société de l'Histoire de Paris et de l'Ile-de-France, vol. 3 (especially the article on the escape from the Bastille by Émile Campardon and Auguste Longnon)

Douarche, A., *Les Tribunaux civils de Paris pendant la Révolution (1791–1800),* (Paris, 1905)

Mémoires et Souvenirs de Charles de Pougens (Paris, 1834)

Légendes et Archives de la Bastille, by F. Funck-Brentano (Paris, 1898) (chap. VI: Latude)

NB Much is owed to Frantz Funck-Brentano. This very serious archivist and Curator of the Arsenal Library did not hesitate to write for the public, combining factual information with a narrative style. We have never hesitated to follow him despite his outright antipathy to Latude. Besides, it is much to F. Funck-Brentano's credit that he was the first, with archival material, to dare to 'depantheonize' a man whom Michelet and Lavisse had extolled as a victim of royal despotism. After him, histriography swung to the other side completely, to the extent that Latude was transformed from an exemplary victim into a 'fieffé filou' (arrant swindler), as F. Ravaisson called him. (The comment by the biographer Jal was equally severe: 'He was treated as the ultimate in wretchedness when he should have been treated as a primary example of madness'.)

As regards the interpretation of Latude's zodiac sign, Pisces, see vol. 12 (Pisces) by André Barbault in the collection *Le Zodiaque* (Seuil: Paris, 1959).

Index

Danry and: plot to gain
favour of *see* parcel;
allegations of witchcraft
90–2, 95, 114; appeals to
16, 20–1, 24–5, 26, 31,
191; invective against 32;
legal proceedings against
heirs 73, 148, 159–60,
166, 168, Memoirs on
174–5, 177; memoranda
against 59, 71, 153, 202–3
death 72–3, 167
in fiction 180–2
Jeanneton Aubespry's letter
to 67
and Maurepas 6–7
popular hatred of 4, 6–7, 8,
174
power over Louis XV 4,
6–7, 159–60
portrait of Danry by Antoine
Vestier 152–3, 154, 191,
200
Pougens, Charles, Chevalier
de 144, 154, 165, 199
prisons 13, 57–8, 123, 124
convents as 13, 66, 57–8
La Désirade 68
Madelonnettes 194
musical instruments in
86–7, 103–4
prisoners' projects 55–6
punishment for escape 53
right to pen and paper
60–1, 86
see also asylums; Bastille;
Bicêtre; Charenton;
Vincennes

projects, prisoners' 55–6
Allègre's 34–5, 64
see also under Danry, Jean
*Proposal for coalition of 83
departments*. . . 162, 168,
203
Protestants 48–9
Prussia 53

Quesnay, François (King's
physician) 7, 20, 24–5,
26, 32–3, 36, 66

rats 54–5
Ravaisson, F. 199
'Rennes' (prisoner in
Charenton) 113
Rennes, magistrate from 88–9
Retz, Cardinal de 170
Revolution 149, 150–61, 172
Revue du théâtre, La 191
rheumatism
Danry 62, 63, 69, 127, 142,
170
Marquis de Fresne 28
Richelieu, Louis François
Armand Duplessis, Duc
de (Marshal) 6, 151
Roanne, Château de 66
Rochebrune, Commissioner
of Bastille 63–4
Rohan, Louis Réné Edouard,
Prince de, Cardinal 131,
132, 197
Romanticism 131–2, 191
Rotterdam 50–2
Rougemont (governor of
Vincennes) 96